JOHN WAYNE
CAST IRON

OFFICIAL COOKBOOK

John Wayne, Charles Coburn and Sigrid Curie in *Three Faces West* (1940). Coburn would win the Academy Award for Best Supporting Actor three years later in *The More the Merrier* (1943).

TRADITION was always important to my father. He understood how essential it was to pass down time-honored rituals to those you loved best. One of the ways that sentiment lives on in my family is through cast-iron cookware. Whether it's a skillet, Dutch oven or grill pan, cast-iron adds a little something extra to every meal—and with proper care, future generations of your family will enjoy using the same cookware you did. We've collected dozens of recipes worthy of what is sure to be your most cherished tool in the kitchen, ranging from mouth-watering sides to hearty main meals and even sweet desserts. We hope they all become part of a new tradition in your family, just like Duke would want.

Ethan Wayne

Duke and his youngest son Ethan on the set of *The War Wagon* (1967). Ethan would often have small roles in his father's films, most notably in *Big Jake* (1971).

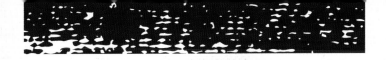

CONTENTS

CAST IRON 101

How to season and clean your cast iron

SEASONING YOUR PAN

Without a good layer of seasoning, a cast-iron pan will eventually start to corrode and rust. Though the initial seasoning (or re-seasoning) can be a lengthy process, your hard work will be well worth it—a properly seasoned pan can be passed down for generations!

If your cast-iron pan is brand new (even if it claims to be pre-seasoned), or getting dull or rusted, it's time to season it.

YOU'LL NEED

Dish soap

Sponge or stiff brush

Paper towels

Vegetable oil or shortening

DIRECTIONS

1. Preheat your oven to 325 degrees F.

2. Wash your skillet with hot, soapy water, scrubbing hard to remove any rust. Usually you should not use soap to clean your cast iron, but it's OK to do this prior to seasoning.

3. Dry your cast-iron pan and wipe it out with paper towels. If any grit comes off on the towels, rewash your pan.

4. Using another paper towel, apply a thin layer of oil or shortening to the inside and outside of your skillet.

5. Place the skillet upside down on your oven's center rack, with a sheet pan or aluminum foil on a rack below it to catch any drips.

6. Bake the pan for 1 hour. Turn off the oven and let the pan cool completely before removing it.

CLEANING YOUR PAN

1. Clean your pan right away, while it's still hot or warm—this is especially important if you've cooked something acidic, like tomatoes. Do not leave it in the sink or let it soak in water, as this may cause rust.

2. Do not use soap, steel wool or a dishwasher to clean your pan. Using a stiff brush or the rough side of a sponge, scrub your pan well and rinse with hot water. Repeat as necessary.

3. To remove extra-stubborn food residue, scrub with salt or boil water in the pan to loosen the food.

4. Once clean, dry your pan on the stove over low heat.

5. While still warm, apply a very light layer of oil on the pan with a paper towel, and then buff to remove any excess oil.

6. Store the skillet in a dry place.

Big Jake's Big
Breakfast Skillet
pg. 18

HEARTY BREAKFASTS

These recipes are doing their part to make mornings great again.

RIO BRAVO BREAKFAST BISCUITS

Like Duke and Dean-O, biscuits and sausage make a winning combo.

**SERVES 8
(2 BISCUITS WITH GRAVY
PER SERVING)**

PROVISIONS

BISCUITS

- 2 cups flour
- 1 Tbsp. baking powder
- 1 tsp. sugar
- 1 tsp. kosher or fine sea salt
- ½ tsp. baking soda
- ½ cup cold butter, cut into small pieces
- 1 cup buttermilk

GRAVY

- 1 lb. breakfast sausage
- ⅓ cup flour
- 4 cups milk
- Salt and pepper, to taste

DIRECTIONS

BISCUITS

1. Preheat oven to 400 degrees F. Line a baking sheet with parchment paper or a silicone baking mat.

2. Place flour, baking powder, sugar, salt and baking soda in a food processor fitted with a steel blade and pulse several times to combine. Add the butter and pulse until the flour resembles coarse meal. Add the buttermilk and process until the mixture forms a dough. Drop the dough in large spoonfuls on the prepared pan—you should get about 16 biscuits. Bake for 17–18 minutes or until golden brown. Split open with a fork or knife and top with gravy.

GRAVY

1. Break the sausage into a cold cast-iron skillet. Turn the heat to medium-high and cook, breaking up the sausage, until browned. Add the flour to the pan and cook for 1 minute, stirring. Add the milk and cook, stirring frequently, until thickened. Season to taste with salt and pepper.

John Wayne and Dean Martin in *Rio Bravo* (1959).

DID YOU KNOW?

John Wayne and Dean Martin starred together in both *Rio Bravo* (1959) and *The Sons of Katie Elder* (1965).

COUNTRY COFFEE CAKE

This crumbly companion to your cup of joe makes any morning a good one.

SERVES 4

PROVISIONS

CAKE
- 2½ cups flour
- 2 tsp. baking powder
- ½ tsp. baking soda
- ½ cup butter, at room temperature plus more for preparing the pan
- 1 cup light brown sugar, packed
- 2 large eggs
- 1 tsp. vanilla extract
- ¾ cup sour cream

TOPPING
- ¾ cup light brown sugar, packed
- ½ cup flour
- 2 tsp. ground cinnamon
- ⅛ tsp. kosher or fine sea salt
- 6 Tbsp. cold butter, cut into small pieces

DIRECTIONS

CAKE
1. Preheat oven to 350 degrees F. Generously grease a 9- to 10-in. cast-iron skillet with butter.

2. Whisk together the flour, baking powder and baking soda in a mixing bowl.

3. In the bowl of an electric mixer, cream together the butter and brown sugar until light and fluffy, about 3 minutes. Add the eggs, one at a time, beating well after each addition. Beat in the vanilla. Turn the mixer to low, add half the flour mixture, then the sour cream and finally the rest of the flour. Beat until everything is just combined. The batter will be stiff. Scrape the batter into the prepared skillet. Prepare the topping and sprinkle it evenly over the cake. Bake for 35 to 40 minutes or until a toothpick inserted into the center comes out clean.

TOPPING
1. Combine the brown sugar, flour, cinnamon and salt in a small mixing bowl. Add the butter and work it into the flour mixture with your fingers until well blended.

John Wayne and son Patrick on the set of *Rio Bravo* (1959).

SEAN THORNTON'S CORNED BEEF HASH FRITTATA

One taste of this hearty breakfast, and your taste buds will be dancing a jig.

SERVES 6 TO 8

PROVISIONS

1 lb. small red potatoes, scrubbed, unpeeled and cut into ½-in. dice

1½ tsp. kosher or fine sea salt

¾ tsp. pepper

10 large eggs

3 Tbsp. heavy cream

1 Tbsp. spicy brown mustard

1 Tbsp. vegetable oil

1 medium white or yellow onion, diced

½ lb. deli corned beef, diced

2 Tbsp. chopped chives

DIRECTIONS

1. Place the potatoes in a microwave-safe bowl with the salt and pepper and stir. Cover the bowl with plastic wrap and microwave on high power for 6 minutes or until tender.

2. Preheat the oven to 400 degrees F.

3. Whisk together the eggs, cream and mustard.

4. Heat oil in a cast-iron skillet over medium until it begins to shimmer. Add onion and cook until tender and translucent, about 5 minutes. Add the potatoes and corned beef. Pour egg mixture over top and use a spatula to make sure eggs surround the potatoes and corned beef. Cook for 1 minute on the stove then transfer the pan to oven. Cook for 12–14 minutes or until the eggs are fully set. Top with chives.

John Wayne and Maureen O'Hara in *The Quiet Man* (1952).

DID YOU KNOW?

Maureen O'Hara testified in front of Congress in 1979 in support of Duke receiving a Congressional Gold Medal.

BIG JAKE'S BIG
BREAKFAST SKILLET

This breakfast brings smiles to the faces of the whole family. Guaranteed.

SERVES 4 TO 6

PROVISIONS

- 6 slices bacon
- 4 cups grated potatoes (from 2–3 large russet potatoes)
- 1 medium white or yellow onion, grated

  Kosher or fine sea salt, to taste

  Pepper, to taste
- 6 large eggs
- 2 cups grated cheddar cheese, divided
- 4 green onions, sliced

DIRECTIONS

1. Preheat oven to 350 degrees F.

2. Place the bacon in a cold, large cast-iron skillet. Turn heat to medium and cook on the stovetop until the bacon is crispy, turning often. Remove the bacon and drain on paper towels. Add the potatoes and onions to the hot bacon grease, add a large pinch of both salt and pepper and stir several times to mix well. Raise the heat to medium-high and cook until the potatoes start to brown on the bottom, about 6 minutes.

3. Whisk the eggs in a mixing bowl, add 1 cup of the cheese and a large pinch of salt and pepper, and stir to combine. Pour the egg mixture over the potatoes, sprinkle the remaining cheese on top, crumble the bacon on top, add the green onions and bake for 10 minutes or until the eggs are set.

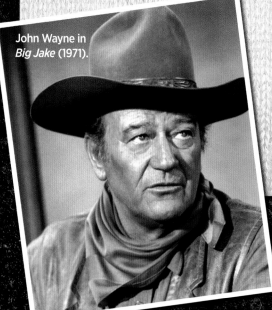

John Wayne in *Big Jake* (1971).

WAYNE FAMILY TIP

To cook your bacon perfectly, add a little bit of water to the pan. It helps cut down on the possibility of burnt bacon.

DUTCH BABY

A man doesn't need to wait until after dinner to enjoy something sweet.
Treat yourself to this puffy pancake you know you deserve.

SERVES 2

PROVISIONS

- 2 large eggs
- ½ cup flour
- ½ cup milk
- ⅛ tsp. kosher or fine sea salt
- 4 Tbsp. butter
- 1 lemon
- Powdered sugar, for serving
- Fresh berries (optional)

DIRECTIONS

1. Place a 9- or 10-in. cast-iron skillet in the oven and preheat the oven to 450 degrees F.

2. Whisk together eggs, flour, milk and salt, beating well. When the oven has heated, carefully remove the pan from the oven, add the butter and swirl the pan to melt the butter and coat the pan. Immediately pour the batter into the pan and return it to the oven. Let bake for 12–15 minutes or until the pancake is puffed and golden brown.

3. Remove the pan from the oven, squeeze the lemon over the pancake, dust with powdered sugar and serve immediately, with berries if desired.

DID YOU KNOW?

The movie *3 Godfathers* is a very loose retelling of the biblical story of the Three Wise Men, transposed to a Western setting.

John Wayne, Harry Carey Jr. and Pedro Armendáriz in a scene from *3 Godfathers* (1948).

FRENCH TOAST CASSEROLE

Might as well unbuckle your belt before tucking into this
breakfast, pilgrim. You'll need the extra room.

SERVES 6 TO 8

PROVISIONS

- 6 large eggs
- 2½ cups milk
- ¼ cup maple syrup, plus more to serve
- 1 tsp. vanilla extract
- 1 tsp. ground cinnamon
- ½ tsp. salt
- 12 slices sandwich bread
- 4 Tbsp. butter, melted

DIRECTIONS

1. In a large mixing bowl, whisk
together the eggs, milk, ¼ cup
maple syrup, vanilla extract,
cinnamon and salt. Cut the bread
into 1-in. cubes. Add the bread to
the egg/milk mixture. Stir gently
to combine. Let sit for 30 minutes,
stirring gently occasionally.

2. Preheat oven to 375 degrees F.

3. Pour the bread mixture into a cast-
iron skillet and gently press down
with a spatula. Top with the melted
butter and bake for 55 minutes or
until golden brown and set. Let
cool for 5 minutes before serving.
Serve with extra maple syrup.

John Wayne with
French model
and actress
Capucine in
North to Alaska
(1960).

John Wayne and son Patrick play chess on the set of *McLintock!* (1963). Patrick went on to have an accomplished acting career of his own and was recently inducted into the The National Cowboy & Western Heritage Museum's Hall of Great Western Performers.

HAM AND EGG SKILLET STRATA

Start the day off right by whipping together this tasty and filling breakfast—there's enough for the whole family!

SERVES 6

PROVISIONS

- 1 Tbsp. vegetable oil
- 1 Tbsp. butter
- 6 slices sandwich bread, cut into 1-in. pieces
- ½ lb. thick sliced deli ham, diced
- 4 green onions, sliced
- 6 large eggs
- 1½ cups milk
- 1 cup grated cheddar cheese
- 1 Tbsp. Worcestershire sauce
- ½ tsp. salt
- ½ tsp. dry mustard
- ½ tsp. pepper

DIRECTIONS

1. Preheat oven to 425 degrees F.

2. Heat a cast-iron skillet over medium heat for 2 minutes. Add the oil and butter. As soon as the butter is melted, add the bread cubes. Toss to coat and cook, stirring occasionally, until the bread is slightly toasted, about 5 minutes. Add the ham and green onions and cook, stirring, for another minute.

3. In a large mixing bowl, whisk together the eggs, milk, cheese, Worcestershire sauce, salt, mustard and pepper. Pour the egg mixture over the bread and press down gently with a spatula.

4. Bake for 20 minutes, or until golden brown and set. Let cool 5 minutes before serving.

John Wayne and Gail Russell in a scene from *Angel and the Badman* (1947).

DID YOU KNOW?

In addition to being a stone-cold classic Western, *Angel and the Badman* is also the first movie produced by John Wayne, who was looking to work behind the camera.

HOME (ON THE RANGE) FRIES

The smell of these potatoes frying in the pan will get 'em out of bed in a hurry.

SERVES 4 TO 6

PROVISIONS

- 2 lb. red potatoes, scrubbed and unpeeled, cut into ¾-in. dice
- 5 Tbsp. vegetable oil, divided
- 1½ tsp. kosher or fine sea salt
- 1 tsp. pepper
- 1 medium white or yellow onion, diced
- 1 red bell pepper, seeded, deveined and diced
- 2 garlic cloves, minced

DIRECTIONS

1. Place the potatoes, 1 Tbsp. oil, salt and pepper in a microwave-safe bowl. Cover with plastic wrap and microwave on high power for 7 to 10 minutes or until tender. Drain well.

2. Heat 2 Tbsp. of oil in a cast-iron skillet over medium until the oil starts to shimmer. Add the onion and red bell pepper and cook, stirring occasionally, until tender and starting to brown. Add the garlic and cook for 30 seconds, stirring. Transfer the mixture to the bowl with the potatoes and mix well.

3. Add the remaining 2 Tbsp. of oil to the now empty skillet and heat until shimmering. Add the potato mixture and flatten it gently with a spatula. Cook, undisturbed, for 5 to 7 minutes or until browned on the bottom.

4. Flip the potatoes, one portion at a time, with a spatula and gently flatten down. Continue to cook, flipping the potatoes every 2 to 3 minutes, until well browned, about 15 minutes. Season to taste with more salt and pepper.

John Wayne with Sam, his canine costar in *Hondo* (1953).

HUEVOS RANCHEROS

Treat yourself to this Southwestern recipe that's almost as classic as Duke himself.

SERVES 2 TO 4

PROVISIONS

- 1 Tbsp. vegetable oil
- 1 small white or yellow onion, diced
- 1 (14.5-oz.) can diced fire roasted tomatoes, undrained
- 1 Tbsp. tomato paste
- 1 (15-oz.) can kidney or pinto beans, rinsed and drained
- 1 (4-oz.) can chopped mild green chilies, drained
- 1 tsp. dried cumin
- ½ tsp. chipotle pepper
- 1 tsp. kosher or fine sea salt, plus more to taste
- ½ tsp. pepper, plus more to taste
- 4 corn tortillas
- 2 Tbsp. butter
- 4 large eggs
- 1 avocado, sliced, to serve
- 2 Tbsp. minced fresh cilantro, to serve

DIRECTIONS

1. Heat oil in a cast-iron skillet over medium-high until it shimmers. Add the onion and cook until tender and translucent, about 4 minutes. Add the tomatoes with the juice and cook for about 1 minute, stirring. Add the tomato paste and cook, stirring for another minute. Add the beans, chilies, cumin, chipotle pepper, 1 tsp. salt and ½ tsp. pepper. Let simmer, uncovered, for about 10 minutes, or until slightly thickened. Keep warm until serving.

2. Heat another cast-iron skillet over medium-high. When hot, add the tortillas, one at a time, and cook until they soften and start to brown in some spots. Remove from skillet and keep warm. Repeat until all tortillas are cooked.

3. Reduce the heat to medium, add the butter and let it melt. Crack the eggs into the skillet, season with salt and pepper and cook 2 to 3 minutes or until desired degree of doneness.

4. To serve, place some of the tomato sauce on a plate, top with an egg, avocado slices and cilantro and serve with the warm tortillas.

Duke on horseback in a scene from *The Undefeated* (1969).

DID YOU KNOW?

John Wayne's costar in *The Undefeated*, Rock Hudson, liked to spend his free time on the set playing chess with the legend.

LOADED BAKED POTATO FRITTATA

Potatoes, bacon and cheese—this meal combines all of Duke's favorites into one delicious meal.

SERVES 6

PROVISIONS

- **6** slices bacon, chopped
- **4** large russet potatoes (about 2 lb.), peeled and cut into 1-in. dice
- **4** green onions, thinly sliced
- **1½ tsp.** kosher or fine sea salt
- **¾ tsp.** pepper
- **8** large eggs
- **2 Tbsp.** milk
- **1** cup grated cheddar cheese, divided

  Sour cream, to serve

DIRECTIONS

1. Preheat oven to 400 degrees F.

2. Place the bacon in a cold cast-iron skillet, turn the heat to medium and cook until crisp, stirring occasionally. Remove with a slotted spoon and drain on paper towels. Leave the bacon grease in the pan.

3. Add the potatoes to the hot bacon grease and cook, stirring occasionally, until tender, about 10 minutes. Reserve about ¼ cup of the green part of the green onions for garnish and add the rest into the pan with the potatoes. Add the bacon, salt and pepper, and stir to mix.

4. Whisk together the eggs, milk and half of the grated cheese. Pour over the potatoes and cook on the stove for about 1 minute or until the eggs just begin to start setting up. Place the pan in the preheated oven and cook for 12 minutes, sprinkle the remaining cheese on top and return to the oven for another 2 minutes or until the cheese is melted and the eggs are fully set.

5. Remove from the oven and let sit for 5 minutes before serving. Cut into wedges and serve topped with sour cream and the reserved green onions.

John Wayne in *The Shootist* (1976).

WAYNE FAMILY
TIP

You can find out if your frittata
is perfectly cooked by placing a
sharp knife in the center. If there's
any raw egg on the knife when
you take it out, stick it back in the
oven for a few minutes.

HOMEMADE BREAKFAST SAUSAGE

These patties are packed with enough flavor to satisfy the pickiest of cowboys.

MAKES 12 SAUSAGES

PROVISIONS

- 1½ lb. ground pork
- 1 small tart apple, such as Granny Smith, peeled, cored and grated
- 1 Tbsp. maple syrup
- 1 Tbsp. minced fresh sage, or 1 tsp. dried sage
- 1 tsp. pepper
- 1 tsp. garlic powder
- ¾ tsp. kosher or fine sea salt
- ¼ tsp. crushed red pepper flakes
- 2 Tbsp. vegetable oil

DIRECTIONS

1. Gently combine pork, apple, maple syrup, sage, pepper, garlic powder, salt and crushed red pepper. Divide the mixture into 12 equal portions, roll into balls and flatten into patties about ½-inch thick.

2. Heat a cast-iron skillet over medium for 5 minutes. Add 1 Tbsp. oil and let it heat until shimmering. Add half the sausage patties and cook 3 to 5 minutes per side or until browned and cooked through. Remove from skillet, place on a paper towel-lined plate and keep warm.

3. Add the remaining Tbsp. oil and repeat with the remaining patties.

John Wayne in *Cahill U.S. Marshal* (1973).

DID YOU KNOW?

Cahill U.S. Marshal was produced by Duke's oldest son Michael, who produced the first of his father's films with *McLintock!* in 1963.

GUNSLINGER SKILLET QUICHE

Whether you eat at the breakfast table or grab a slice to go,
this pastry will keep you sated until lunch.

SERVES 6

PROVISIONS

- 1 recipe piecrust (recipe follows) or pre-made piecrust
- 6 large eggs
- 2 cups half-and-half
- 1 cup grated cheddar cheese
- 1 tsp. kosher or fine sea salt
- ½ tsp. pepper
- 1 cup cherry tomatoes, halved

PIECRUST

- ½ cup unsalted butter
- 2–4 Tbsp. water
- 1¼ cup flour
- 1 tsp. kosher or fine sea salt
- 2 Tbsp. sugar

DIRECTIONS

1. Preheat oven to 375 degrees F.

2. Grease a 10-in. cast-iron skillet. Line the skillet with the piecrust. Tuck outer ½ in. of the dough underneath itself to form an edge. Prick the bottom of the crust in several places with a fork.

3. Place a double layer of tin foil over the crust, line with pie weights or dried beans and bake for 25 to 30 minutes or until pale brown.

4. Remove the skillet from the oven, carefully remove the pie weights and foil, and reduce the oven temperature to 350 degrees F.

5. In a large mixing bowl, whisk together the eggs, half-and-half, cheese, salt and pepper.

6. Place the cherry tomatoes halves in the bottom of the piecrust. Pour the egg mixture over and bake for 35 minutes or until set. Let cool 5 minutes before serving.

PIECRUST

1. Cut the butter into ½-in. pieces and place in the freezer for 15 to 30 minutes. Add some ice cubes to the water and let it get ice cold while preparing the dry ingredients.

2. Combine the flour, salt and sugar in the bowl of a food processor. Add the butter and pulse until the flour resembles coarse meal with some pea-sized pieces of butter. With the processor running, add the water, 1 Tbsp. at a time, until the mixture just begins to clump together.

3. Remove the dough from the machine, form into a disk and wrap in plastic wrap. Refrigerate for 30 minutes before rolling out on a floured board.

Duke and Claire Trevor in *Allegheny Uprising* (1939).

Skillet
Hasselback
Potatoes
pg. 49

SLAMMIN' SIDES

No meal is complete without one of these recipes.

BACONY BAKED BEANS

How do you make a cowboy classic even better? Just add bacon.

SERVES 10 TO 12

PROVISIONS

- 1 lb. dried white beans
- 6 slices thick cut bacon, chopped
- 1 large white or yellow onion, diced
- 1 jalapeño pepper, seeded, deveined and minced
- 1 cup barbecue sauce
- ½ cup light brown sugar, packed
- ¼ cup ketchup
- ¼ cup apple cider vinegar
- 1 tsp. dry mustard

DIRECTIONS

1. Place the beans in a large bowl, cover with water and soak overnight. Drain and rinse the beans, place in a cast-iron Dutch oven, cover with fresh water, bring to a boil, reduce the heat, cover the pot and simmer for 2 hours. Drain the beans.

2. Preheat oven to 325 degrees F.

3. Rinse and dry the Dutch oven, put back on the stove over medium heat, add the bacon and cook, stirring occasionally, until cooked through but not crispy. Add the onion and cook, stirring occasionally, until tender, about 5 minutes. Add the jalapeño pepper and cook, stirring, for one minute. Add the beans back to the pot along with the rest of the ingredients. Cook for 2 to 3 minutes, stirring.

4. Put the lid on the Dutch oven and bake for 2 hours or until the sauce is the consistency of syrup. Let sit for a few minutes before serving, if desired.

John Wayne in *Red River* (1948).

DID YOU KNOW?

John Wayne and legendary director Howard Hawks made five films together, starting with Red River in 1948.

MAPLE BACON
BRUSSELS SPROUTS

Hold it right there, pilgrim! You've just discovered the perfect side for any occasion.

SERVES 4 TO 6

PROVISIONS

- 4 slices thick cut bacon
- 2 Tbsp. butter
- 1 lb. Brussels sprouts, trimmed and cut in half
- 3 Tbsp. maple syrup
- Kosher or fine sea salt, to taste
- Pepper, to taste

DIRECTIONS

1. Slice the bacon widthwise into ¼-in. strips. Place in a cold cast-iron skillet, turn the heat to medium and cook, stirring occasionally, until crisp. Remove from the skillet with a slotted spoon and drain on paper towels.

2. Add the butter to the pan, let the butter melt, then add the Brussels sprouts. Cook, stirring occasionally, until fork tender. Add the maple syrup and bacon, and cook for another 30 to 60 seconds, stirring to coat the Brussels sprouts with the maple syrup. Season to taste with salt and pepper.

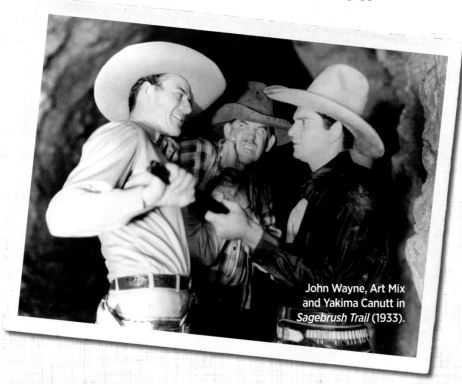

John Wayne, Art Mix and Yakima Canutt in *Sagebrush Trail* (1933).

APPLE CHEESE SKILLET BREAD

This savory side is perfect for helping soak up every last bit of flavor on your plate.

SERVES 6 TO 8

PROVISIONS

Butter, for greasing pan

2½ cups flour

2 Tbsp. sugar

4 tsp. baking powder

1 tsp. kosher or fine sea salt

2 cups grated cheddar cheese

12 oz. sparkling apple cider

DIRECTIONS

1. Preheat oven to 450 degrees F and generously grease a cast-iron skillet.

2. In a large mixing bowl, combine the flour, sugar, baking powder and salt. Reserve about ½ cup of grated cheese and stir the rest into the flour, making sure to coat the cheese with the flour mixture. Stir in the apple cider.

3. Spread the batter into the prepared pan, sprinkle the reserved cheese evenly over the top and bake for 20 to 25 minutes or until a toothpick inserted in the center comes out clean.

4. Let cool in the pan for 15 minutes before removing to a wire rack to finish cooling.

John Smith, John Wayne and Claudia Cardinale in *Circus World* (1964).

DID YOU KNOW?

Most of the filming for *Circus World* took place in Europe, which gave Duke an excellent excuse to sail around on his newly acquired boat, the *Wild Goose*.

BLISTERED GREEN BEANS & TOMATOES

One helping of this side dish, and you'll never
hear 'em complain about eating their vegetables again.

SERVES 4

PROVISIONS

- 1   Tbsp. olive oil
- 2   Tbsp. butter
- 1   lb. green beans, trimmed
- 1½ cups cherry or grape tomatoes, halved
- 2   garlic cloves, minced
- 1   Tbsp. balsamic vinegar
-     Kosher or fine sea salt, to taste
-     Pepper, to taste

DIRECTIONS

1. Heat a cast-iron skillet over medium-high for 3 minutes. Add the oil and butter and, when the butter has melted, the green beans, tomatoes and garlic. Let sit for 90 seconds, undisturbed. Toss and cook for another 2 to 3 minutes or until the beans are crisp tender and the tomatoes start breaking down. Add the vinegar, toss to coat, season to taste with salt and pepper and serve.

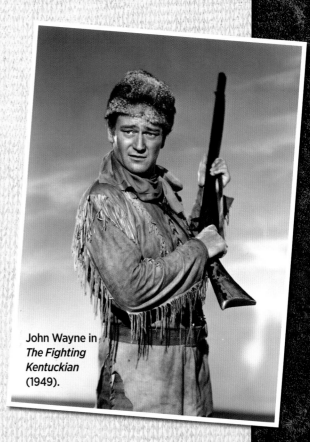

John Wayne in
*The Fighting
Kentuckian*
(1949).

WAYNE FAMILY TIP

You don't want to eat the tough ends of green beans you bring home from the store. Line up all of the beans so the ends are grouped together, and cut them off with a knife prior to cooking.

SKILLET HASSELBACK POTATOES

This no-frills potato dish is guaranteed to become an instant favorite from your first bite.

SERVES 6

PROVISIONS

- 6   medium Idaho potatoes
- ½   cup butter, melted
- ¼   cup olive oil
- 6   Tbsp. chopped chives
- 2   tsp. kosher or fine sea salt
- 1   tsp. pepper

DIRECTIONS

1. Preheat oven to 450 degrees F.

2. Scrub the potatoes and slice them into thin slices, leaving the bottom ¼ in. uncut. Place the potatoes in a cast-iron skillet.

3. Combine the melted butter, olive oil, chives, salt and pepper. Brush the potatoes with the mixture, making sure to get it down in between the slices. Save a little bit of the butter mixture to brush on after the potatoes are done baking.

4. Bake for 1 hour or until tender. Brush with the reserved butter mixture and serve.

John Wayne in *The Comancheros* (1961).

DID YOU KNOW?

Despite being a globe-trotting celebrity who could dine at the finest of establishments, Duke never strayed from his humble roots as a "meat and potatoes" guy.

HONDO'S HUSH PUPPIES WITH SPICY HONEY BUTTER

A man oughta do what he thinks is right—and that includes chowing down on this sweet and spicy side.

MAKES 30 TO 36 HUSH PUPPIES

PROVISIONS

- 6 Tbsp. butter, softened
- 3 Tbsp. honey
- 1–2 tsp. Sriracha sauce
- 1½ cups cornmeal
- 1 cup flour
- 1 Tbsp. baking powder
- 1 Tbsp. sugar
- 1 tsp. baking soda
- 1 tsp. salt, plus more for sprinkling
- 4 green onions, finely chopped
- 1½ cups buttermilk
- 2 large eggs
- 4 cups vegetable oil or shortening

DIRECTIONS

1. Combine the butter, honey and Sriracha sauce in a small bowl and mix well. Put in a small serving dish.

2. In a large mixing bowl, whisk together the cornmeal, flour, baking powder, sugar, baking soda and 1 tsp. salt. Add the green onions, buttermilk and eggs, then stir well.

3. Turn the oven on warm. Line a baking sheet with paper towels.

4. Heat the vegetable oil or shortening in a cast-iron skillet until it reaches 375 degrees F. Drop tablespoonfuls of batter (a small ice cream scoop works well for this) into the hot oil, being careful not to overcrowd the pan. Fry until golden brown on one side, 2 to 4 minutes, flip and fry until golden brown on the other side. Remove the hushpuppies from the oil with a slotted spoon and place on the prepared baking sheet. Sprinkle with a tiny bit of salt. Keep them warm in the oven until you finish frying all the batter. Serve with spicy honey butter.

John Wayne in *Hondo* (1953).

PAN FRIED KALE

This side dish is packed with enough oil, garlic and salt to turn the toughest of kale skeptics into true believers.

SERVES 4

PROVISIONS

- 1 bunch kale
- 4 large garlic cloves
- 1 Tbsp. olive oil
- 1 tsp. kosher or fine sea salt, plus more to taste
- 2 Tbsp. fresh lemon juice (from ½ lemon)
- ¼ tsp. crushed red pepper

DIRECTIONS

1. Remove the stems from the kale, wash the leaves and dry well. Coarsely chop the kale. Smash the garlic cloves with the side of a knife and discard the skins.

2. Heat a cast-iron skillet on high for 3 minutes. Add the oil and garlic to the pan and cook for 30 seconds. Add as much kale as will fit in the pan along with 1 tsp. salt. Using a pair of tongs, turn the kale in the pan to wilt slightly. Add more kale, in batches, until it is all in the pan. Continue to cook until the kale is tender and the garlic is golden brown but not burned, about 5 minutes. Add the lemon juice and red pepper and toss to coat. Taste and add more salt, if desired.

John Wayne and Robert Mitchum in *El Dorado* (1967).

DID YOU KNOW?

El Dorado's screenwriter, Leigh Brackett, also penned scripts for the Duke classic *Rio Bravo* (1959) as well as a draft for the sci-fi blockbuster *The Empire Strikes Back* (1980).

SKILLET-STYLE MEXICAN STREET CORN

One spoonful of this flavorful side dish is like treating your tastebuds to a well-deserved fiesta.

SERVES 4

PROVISIONS

- 1 Tbsp. olive oil
- 4 cups fresh or frozen (and thawed) corn kernels
- 1 (10-oz.) can diced tomatoes and green chilies, drained
- ¾ cup grated Cotija cheese, divided
- ½ cup mayonnaise
- Zest of 1 lime, finely grated
- ¼ cup fresh cilantro leaves, coarsely chopped
- Lime wedges, to serve

DIRECTIONS

1. Heat the oil in a cast-iron skillet until it shimmers. Add the corn and spread into an even layer. Cook, stirring and smoothing back into an even layer occasionally, until the corn starts to brown, about 5 minutes. Add the canned tomatoes and green chilies and cook, stirring, for 1 minute. Add ½ cup cheese, mayonnaise and lime zest, and cook for another minute, stirring. Stir in the cilantro leaves, top with the remaining cheese and serve with lime wedges.

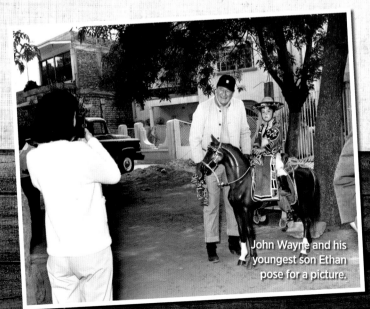

John Wayne and his youngest son Ethan pose for a picture.

PAN-SEARED ARTICHOKE HEARTS

This tender and tangy side dish will make any meal one to remember.

SERVES 4

PROVISIONS

- 5   Tbsp. olive oil, divided
- 1   Tbsp. sherry or red wine vinegar
- 1   tsp. Italian seasoning
- 1   tsp. salt
- ½   tsp. pepper
- 2   (10-oz.) boxes frozen artichoke hearts, thawed
- 1   Tbsp. butter
- 2   Tbsp. fresh lemon juice (from ½ a lemon)
- ¼   cup chopped Italian parsley (chopped then measured)
- 1   oz. Parmesan cheese

DIRECTIONS

1. Whisk together 3 Tbsp. olive oil with the vinegar, Italian seasoning, salt and pepper.

2. Add the artichoke hearts and toss to coat.

3. Heat the remaining olive oil in a cast-iron skillet over medium-high until it starts to shimmer.

4. Add the artichokes in a single layer and cook until charred, 3 to 5 minutes per side. Add the butter to the pan. As soon as the butter melts, take the pan off the heat and add the lemon juice and parsley and stir.

5. Grate the Parmesan over the warm artichokes before serving.

John Wayne in a scene from *Legend of the Lost* (1957).

DID YOU KNOW?

The film *Legend of the Lost* was directed by Henry Hathaway, who also helmed the film in which Duke turned in an Oscar-winning performance— *True Grit* (1969).

MASHED POTATO CASSEROLE

Try a new twist on an old classic with this can't-miss casserole!

SERVES 10 TO 12

PROVISIONS

- 2 Tbsp. plus 1 tsp. kosher or fine sea salt, divided
- 6 lb. Yukon gold potatoes, peeled and cut into chunks
- 14 Tbsp. unsalted butter, plus more for preparing the pan, divided
- 1½ cups sour cream
- 2 large eggs, lightly beaten
- 1 tsp. pepper
- 6 Tbsp. finely chopped chives
- ⅔ cup panko breadcrumbs
- ⅔ cup Parmesan cheese

DIRECTIONS

1. Combine 4 quarts water, 2 Tbsp. salt and the potatoes in a large pot. Bring to a boil and cook until the potatoes are fork tender, about 20 minutes. Drain the potatoes, add back to the hot pan and cook, stirring until the potatoes stop steaming.

2. Preheat oven to 400 degrees F. Grease a cast-iron Dutch oven with butter.

3. Mash the potatoes with 10 Tbsp. butter, sour cream, eggs, 1 tsp. salt and pepper. Stir in the chives. Spread the potatoes into the prepared Dutch oven.

4. Melt 4 Tbsp. butter and combine with the breadcrumbs and cheese. Sprinkle the mixture over the top and bake for 30 to 40 minutes or until golden brown.

Duke with the cast of *McLintock!* (1963).

WAYNE FAMILY
TIP

If you're worried you can't polish off this dish in one go, consider adding a little extra butter when mashing the potatoes—it will help the recipe retain its appetizing texture after freezing and reheating it.

John Wayne and Claire Trevor on the set of *Stagecoach* (1939). Trevor made her home in Newport Beach, California, years before Duke himself settled there.

WAYNE FAMILY TIP

Remember to cut these vegetables into even-sized pieces, per the recipe! Otherwise, you'll have a mix of burnt and under-cooked veggies.

ROOSTER'S ROASTED ROOT VEGETABLES

When the hefty marshal in your life needs to cut back
on the pounds without sacrificing taste, reach for this recipe.

SERVES 6

PROVISIONS

- 4 large carrots, peeled and cut into 1-in. pieces
- 2 medium Idaho potatoes (½–¾ lb. each), peeled and cut into 1-in. cubes
- 2 medium sweet potatoes (½–¾ lb. each), peeled and cut into 1-in. cubes
- 3 medium beets, peeled and cut into 1-in. cubes
- 4 small onions, peeled and cut in half lengthwise
- 1 head garlic, cloves separated, peeled and left whole
- 3 Tbsp. olive oil
- 2 tsp. kosher or fine sea salt
- 1 tsp. pepper

DIRECTIONS

1. Preheat oven to 400 degrees F.

2. Put all the vegetables in a cast-iron skillet. Drizzle with the olive oil and sprinkle the salt and pepper over. Toss to coat. Bake for 45 minutes or until the vegetables are tender, stirring the vegetables every 15 minutes.

John Wayne in
Rooster Cogburn
(1975).

SKILLET SCALLOPED POTATOES

Keep your eye on this creamy side dish—family and friends
might gobble it up while your back's turned.

SERVES 6 TO 8

PROVISIONS

2 Tbsp. butter, plus more for preparing
the pan

4 large Idaho potatoes (3 ½–4 lb.),
peeled and very thinly sliced

Kosher or fine sea salt, to taste

Pepper, to taste

2 cups heavy cream, divided

DIRECTIONS

1. Preheat oven to 375 degrees F.
Grease a 9- to 10-in. cast-iron skillet
generously with butter. Arrange
an even layer of potatoes in the
skillet. Sprinkle with a large pinch
of salt and pepper and drizzle with
3 Tbsp. cream. Repeat layers until
all the potatoes are used. Pour
any remaining cream over the top
and press down on the potatoes to
submerge them in cream. Cut 2 Tbsp.
butter into small pieces and scatter
over the top.

2. Cover the pan with foil and bake for
30 minutes. Remove the foil and
bake for another 30 to 45 minutes
or until all the cream has been
absorbed, the potatoes are tender and
the top is golden brown.

John Wayne and
Ward Bond play
cards in a scene
from *Tall in the
Saddle* (1944).

WAYNE FAMILY TIP

If you feel particularly adventurous, add a layer of your favorite cheese (grated) to the potatoes before cooking. You'll know it's chow time when the cheese turns golden brown.

SCALLOPED TOMATOES

You say "tomato." I say "tomahto." But we can both agree to say "delicious" when describing this dish.

SERVES 6

PROVISIONS

- 2 lb. plum tomatoes
- 1 Tbsp. minced fresh rosemary
- 2 Tbsp. balsamic vinegar
- 2 Tbsp. olive oil
- 5 garlic cloves, minced or grated
- 2 tsp. kosher or fine sea salt
- 1 tsp. freshly ground black pepper
- 1¼ cups panko style breadcrumbs, divided
- ½ cup grated Parmesan cheese
- 2 Tbsp. melted butter

DIRECTIONS

1. Preheat oven to 350 degrees F.

2. Cut the tomatoes into roughly 1-in. pieces. Place in greased 9-inch cast-iron skillet. Add the rosemary, balsamic vinegar, olive oil, minced garlic cloves, salt, pepper and 1 cup of the breadcrumbs, and toss well. Bake for 25 minutes.

3. Combine the remaining ¼ cup of breadcrumbs with the Parmesan cheese, top the tomatoes, and cook for 10 more minutes or until the top is nicely browned.

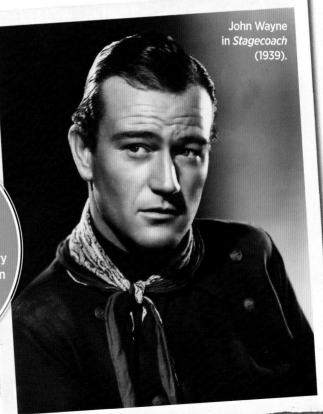

John Wayne in *Stagecoach* (1939).

DID YOU KNOW?

When he was a youngster, John Wayne helped his father try to raise crops on a homestead in California's Mojave Desert. Talk about a real pioneer!

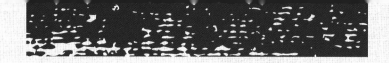

SOUTHERN CORNBREAD

This crumbly treat goes well with any meal...or even without one!

SERVES 8 TO 10

PROVISIONS

- 1⅓ cups yellow or white cornmeal
- 1⅓ cups flour
- 1½ tsp. baking powder
- ½ tsp. baking soda
- ½ tsp. fine sea salt
- 1½ cups buttermilk
- ⅓ cup sugar
- 3 large eggs, lightly beaten
- 8 Tbsp. melted unsalted butter, divided

DIRECTIONS

1. Place a 9- or 10-in. cast-iron skillet in the oven and preheat the oven to 400 degrees F.

2. Combine the cornmeal, flour, baking powder, baking soda and salt in a mixing bowl. Whisk to combine.

3. In a separate bowl, whisk together the buttermilk, sugar, eggs and 6 Tbsp. melted butter. Add the wet ingredients to the dry and stir to combine.

4. Carefully remove the skillet from the oven, add 2 Tbsp. butter to the pan and swirl to coat. Pour in the batter, smooth the top and bake for 30 minutes or until golden brown and a toothpick inserted into the center comes out clean. Let cool in the pan for 10 minutes.

John Wayne in *The Horse Soldiers* (1959).

SUMMER SQUASH GRATIN

Squash your hunger pangs with this cheesy bit of deliciousness.

SERVES 4 TO 6

PROVISIONS

- 2–2½ lb. summer squash (zucchini and yellow squash)
- 3 slices stale sandwich bread
- ⅓ cup olive oil
- 4 anchovy filets
- 3 Tbsp. butter
- 3 garlic cloves, minced
- 1 tsp. kosher or fine sea salt
- ½ tsp. pepper
- ½ cup chopped Italian parsley
- ⅓ cup grated Parmesan cheese
- 2 large shallots, thinly sliced
- 1 cup grated Gruyère cheese, grated

DIRECTIONS

1. Preheat oven to 400 degrees F.

2. Thinly slice the squash (⅛–¼-in. thick) and place in a bowl with the salt. Let sit for 10 minutes. Drain the squash and lay on paper towels to dry, patting the top of the squash dry. Let dry while preparing the breadcrumbs.

3. Place the bread in a food processor or blender and grind into crumbs. Heat the oil in a cast-iron skillet over medium. Add the anchovies and cook, mashing with a spatula, until they melt into the oil, about 5 minutes. Add the butter and let it melt. Lower the heat and add the garlic, salt and pepper and cook, stirring, for 1 minute. Stir in the breadcrumbs and cook, stirring occasionally, until they are golden brown and fragrant. Remove from the skillet to a small bowl and let cool about 10 minutes. Stir in the parsley and Parmesan cheese.

4. In a mixing bowl, combine the squash, shallots, Gruyère cheese and half of the breadcrumbs. Stir to combine.

5. Wipe out the skillet you made the breadcrumbs in and put in the squash mixture. Scatter the remaining breadcrumbs over the top and bake for 30 to 40 minutes or until the squash is tender and the breadcrumbs are browned and crisp.

John Wayne in
Riders of Destiny
(1933).

DID YOU KNOW?

Throughout his career, John Wayne had several horses he would use in multiple films, such as Starlight (pictured above), which he rode again in 1934's *West of the Divide*.

CHARRED SUMMER VEGETABLE SALAD

This medley of perfectly-prepared veggies is sure
to keep you cool on even the hottest days.

SERVES 4 TO 6

PROVISIONS

- 5 Tbsp. olive oil, divided
- 1 Tbsp. sherry vinegar
- ½ tsp. kosher or fine sea salt, plus more to taste
- ¼ tsp. pepper, plus more to taste
- 2 cups fresh or frozen (and thawed) corn kernels
- 2 zucchini cut into ½-in. dice
- 1 red or yellow bell pepper, seeded, deveined and cut into ½-in. dice
- 1 medium sweet onion, diced
- 1 garlic clove, minced
- 2 tomatoes, seeded and diced
- ¼ cup fresh basil leaves, chopped

Laurence Harvey, Richard
Widmark and John Wayne lead
the defense in *The Alamo* (1960).

DIRECTIONS

1. Make the dressing by whisking together 3 Tbsp. oil with the vinegar, ½ tsp. salt and ¼ tsp. of pepper. Set aside.

2. Heat a cast-iron skillet over high for 5 minutes. Add remaining oil and heat until it starts to smoke. Add the corn, zucchini, bell pepper and onion and cook, stirring occasionally, until the vegetables are crisp tender and starting to brown, about 5 minutes. Add the garlic and cook, stirring, for 30 seconds. Add the dressing, stir to combine then remove the skillet from the heat. Transfer the vegetables to a bowl and let cool.

3. Once the vegetables have cooled to room temperature, add the tomatoes and basil. Stir to combine. Season to taste with additional salt and pepper if needed. Can be served at room temperature or cold.

Braised Chicken
Thighs with Root
Vegetables pg. 129

MAIN EVENTS

From steaks to chops and everything in between, these meals are why you bought your cast iron.

OVEN-BRAISED BRISKET

A big helping of this brisket is the perfect way to end the day.

SERVES 6

PROVISIONS

- 2 Tbsp. chili powder
- 1 Tbsp. paprika
- 1 Tbsp. garlic powder
- 1 Tbsp. onion powder
- 1 Tbsp. brown sugar
- 1 Tbsp. kosher or fine sea salt
- 1 Tbsp. pepper
- 2 tsp. dry mustard
- 1 (3- to 4-lb.) flat brisket, trimmed
- 4 Tbsp. olive oil, divided
- 3 large white or yellow onions, thinly sliced
- 1–1 ½ cups beef broth

DIRECTIONS

1. Combine the chili powder, paprika, garlic powder, onion powder, brown sugar, salt, pepper and mustard in a small bowl. Spread the spice mixture all over the brisket, pressing it into the meat. Let the meat sit at room temperature for 30 minutes.

2. Preheat oven to 350 degrees F. Heat 2 Tbsp. oil in a cast-iron Dutch oven large enough to hold the brisket. Brown the brisket well on both sides. Remove to a plate. Add 2 more Tbsp. of oil and let it heat up. Add the onions and scrape up the brown bits from the bottom of the pan. Lower the heat to medium and cook, stirring occasionally, until the onions are very soft and have caramelized, about 15 minutes. Place the brisket on top of the onions and bake uncovered for 1 hour.

3. Lower the oven temperature to 300 degrees F, add 1 cup beef broth to the Dutch oven, cover and bake for another 3 hours or until the brisket is very tender. Check the pot periodically and if it is getting too dry, add a little more beef broth.

Duke in *The Man Who Shot Liberty Valance* (1962).

DID YOU KNOW?

Duke amassed an impressive arsenal of firearms during his lifetime, many of which he donated to The National Cowboy & Western Heritage Museum in Oklahoma City.

CAST-IRON SKILLET STEAKS

There're a few things you can always count on: death, taxes and the delicious flavor of a steak done right.

SERVES 2

PROVISIONS

- 2 boneless steaks such as flat iron, hanger or outside skirt, 1-in. thick and about ½ lb. each
- ½ tsp. kosher or coarse sea salt
- 4 Tbsp. unsalted butter
- 2 garlic cloves, peeled and lightly smashed
- 4 sprigs fresh thyme or oregano
- Pepper, to taste

DIRECTIONS

1. Remove steaks from refrigerator 30 to 60 minutes before planning to cook. Place on a paper towel-lined plate. Flip the steaks occasionally and change the paper towel if needed. The purpose is to really dry out the steaks.

2. Place a cast-iron skillet on the stove over high heat. Sprinkle ½ tsp. of salt evenly over the bottom of the pan and let the pan heat for 10 minutes. Pat steaks dry again, place in the pan and cook for 1 minute. Using tongs, flip the steaks over and rub on bottom of pan to get salt on second side, cook for 30 seconds. Flip again, cook for 30 seconds, then add the butter, garlic and thyme or oregano to pan. Cook the steaks for 2 to 3 more minutes, flipping every 30 seconds. Internal temperature should be between 120 and 125 degrees F for medium rare. Remove steaks from skillet, sprinkle with a pinch of pepper, and let rest 5 minutes before slicing.

John Wayne in *El Dorado* (1967).

CHIPOTLE FLANK STEAK

The south-of-the-border spices help bring a new taste to a classic cut of meat.

SERVES 6

PROVISIONS

- ½   cup orange juice
- ½   cup honey
-      Juice of 2 limes
- ½   cup chopped cilantro leaves
- 3   garlic cloves, grated
- 3   Tbsp. Dijon mustard
- 1   chipotle in adobo sauce, minced, with 1 Tbsp. sauce
- 2   tsp. ground cumin
- 2   tsp. kosher or fine sea salt
- 1   tsp. pepper
- 1 ½–2 lb. flank steak
- 1   Tbsp. cold butter

DIRECTIONS

1. Combine the orange juice, honey, lime juice, cilantro, garlic, mustard, chipotle in adobo and sauce, cumin, salt and pepper in a mixing bowl and whisk together. Put the steak in a large food storage bag, pour in the marinade and let marinate at room temperature for 1 hour or in the refrigerator for 4 to 8 hours.

2. Remove the steak from the marinade, pour the marinade into a sauce pan, pat the steak dry, and let come to room temperature if refrigerated. Bring the marinade to a boil. Continue to boil the marinade while the steak cooks and rests until it reduces to ¼ cup. Take off the heat and stir in the butter until it melts.

3. Preheat a cast-iron grill pan over high heat for 5 minutes. Spray the pan with nonstick cooking spray. Place the steak on the hot grill pan and cook, undisturbed, for 4 minutes. Flip and cook for another 4 minutes or until desired doneness. Take off the grill pan and let rest 5 to 10 minutes before slicing. Slice the meat against the grain. Serve with the sauce, lime and orange wedges and fresh cilantro if desired.

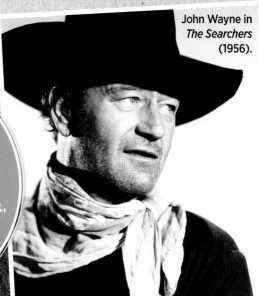

John Wayne in *The Searchers* (1956).

DID YOU KNOW?

One of John Wayne's favorite places to grab a steak in his home of Newport Beach, California, was "A" Restaurant, an establishment still open today!

ALL-AMERICAN BURGER

This isn't just the burger you need. It's the one you deserve. Eat up!

SERVES 4
PROVISIONS

- 1 ½ lb. ground chuck
- Kosher or fine sea salt, to taste
- Pepper, to taste
- 2 Tbsp. vegetable oil
- 4 slices American cheese
- 4 hamburger buns
- Ketchup, to serve
- Mustard, to serve
- Lettuce, to serve
- Tomatoes, to serve
- Dill chip pickles, to serve

DIRECTIONS

1. Place a cast-iron skillet in the oven and heat to 500 degrees F.

2. Divide the ground chuck into 4 equal-sized portions. Loosely form each portion into a patty ¾-in. thick. Make a deep impression in the center of each patty and season generously with salt and pepper on both sides. Place in the refrigerator while the oven heats up.

3. When the oven reaches 500 degrees F, carefully remove the skillet and place on the stove over medium-high heat and turn off the oven.

4. Add the oil to the pan and heat until it shimmers. Add the patties and cook until the burgers are golden brown and slightly charred, about 3 minutes. Flip the burgers and cook for 3 minutes. Add a slice of cheese to each burger, place a lid or another skillet over the pan, and cook for another minute or two or until the bottom of the burgers are golden brown and slightly charred and the cheese has melted.

5. Serve on buns with fixings on the side so each diner can build their perfect burger.

John Wayne and Dean Martin in *The Sons of Katie Elder* (1965).

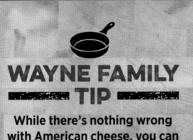

COWBOY NACHOS

One taste of these spicy nachos will get your spurs jinglin' and janglin'!

SERVES 6 TO 8

PROVISIONS

1	recipe Sloppy Jakes (see page 103) without buns
1	(12-oz.) bag corn tortilla chips
1	(15-oz.) can black beans, rinsed and drained
1	cup grated mozzarella cheese
1	cup grated cheddar cheese
½	cup salsa
¼	cup pickled jalapeño slices

DIRECTIONS

1. Heat up the sloppy joes if not already warm.

2. Put a large cast-iron skillet in the oven and preheat the oven to 350 degrees F. When the oven has preheated, carefully remove the skillet and fill with the tortilla chips. Pour the sloppy joes over the chips, then add the beans and sprinkle the cheeses evenly over the top. Bake for 8 to 10 minutes or until the cheese melts.

3. Top with the salsa and jalapeño slices. Serve immediately.

John Wayne in *The Cowboys* (1972).

DID YOU KNOW?

Rodeo star and Western actor Slim Pickens also had a role in Duke's 1972 film *The Cowboys*. Pickens would star in comedian Mel Brooks's Western satire *Blazing Saddles* two years later.

NORTH TO ALASKA MEATLOAF

This hearty dish will warm both your body and soul for even the coldest of journeys.

SERVES 6

PROVISIONS

MEATLOAF

- 1 lb. ground chuck
- 1 lb. ground pork
- 1 medium white or yellow onion
- ¾ cup fresh breadcrumbs (from 2 slices of stale bread, ground)
- ⅔ cup milk
- 1 large egg
- 4 Tbsp. ketchup
- 3 Tbsp. Worcestershire sauce
- 1½ tsp. kosher or fine sea salt
- 1 tsp. garlic powder
- ¾ tsp. pepper

SAUCE

- ½ cup ketchup
- 3 Tbsp. apple cider vinegar
- 3 Tbsp. brown sugar

DIRECTIONS

1. Preheat oven to 350 degrees F. Line the bottom of a cast-iron or enameled cast-iron Dutch oven with a piece of parchment paper.

2. Combine the meats in a large mixing bowl. Grate the onion over the meat with a box grater. Add the rest of the meatloaf ingredients and mix lightly with a fork, being careful not to mash the ingredients together. Shape the mixture into a loaf shape on top of the parchment paper.

3. Combine the sauce ingredients and pour over the meatloaf. Cover the Dutch oven and bake for 1 hour to 1 hour 15 minutes.

4. Pour the sauce out of the pan into a large glass measuring cup. Keep the Dutch oven covered and let the meatloaf sit while reducing the sauce. Skim off as much fat from the sauce as possible, pour into a saucepan and bring to a boil. Let boil for 6 to 7 minutes or until reduced and thick.

5. Remove the meatloaf with a large spatula to a serving plate and top with the sauce.

Duke in a scene from *North to Alaska* (1960).

PERFECT PORTERHOUSE STEAK

Once John Wayne could afford steak, he never went back.
Once you try this steak, you'll never settle for less, either.

SERVES 2

PROVISIONS

- 1 (2-in. thick) porterhouse steak
- Kosher or fine sea salt, to taste
- Pepper, to taste
- 1 Tbsp. vegetable oil
- 4 whole garlic cloves, peeled
- 4 sprigs fresh rosemary
- 3 Tbsp. butter

John Wayne and
Katharine Hepburn in
Rooster Cogburn (1975).

DIRECTIONS

1. Remove steak from refrigerator and let sit at room temperature for 30 minutes.

2. Preheat oven to 500 degrees F.

3. Pat the steak dry with paper towels and season liberally with salt and pepper on both sides.

4. Heat a cast-iron skillet on the stove over medium-high, add the oil, garlic and rosemary and heat until the oil starts to smoke. Remove and discard the garlic and rosemary. Place the steak in the center of the pan and let it cook without moving it for 4 minutes. Flip the steak over, put the butter on top and place in the preheated oven. Let it cook for another 5 to 6 minutes or until it reaches an internal temperature of 125 degrees F (for medium-rare). Remove from the oven, take the steak from the pan and let it rest for 5 to 10 minutes before serving.

DID YOU KNOW?

Rooster Cogburn is the only time John Wayne starred in a sequel to one of his major motion pictures, and also the only time he worked with Katharine H...

HERB-CRUSTED SKIRT STEAK

When you want to dress up your steak in some tortillas, reach for this recipe.

SERVES 6 TO 8

PROVISIONS

- 1 cup (packed) flat leaf parsley
- 1 cup (packed) basil leaves
- 2 bunches green onions, divided
- 2 Tbsp. coarsely chopped pickled jalapeño peppers
- 1 Tbsp. jalapeño pickling liquid
- 2 garlic cloves, chopped
- ¼ cup olive oil
- 1½ tsp. kosher or fine sea salt
- 1 tsp. pepper
- 2½ lb. skirt steak
- Vegetable oil

FOR SERVING

- Corn tortillas, warmed
- Prepared salsa verde
- Avocado slices
- Lime wedges

DIRECTIONS

1. Place the parsley, basil, 3 chopped green onions, jalapeño, pickling liquid, garlic, olive oil, salt and pepper in a food processor and process, scraping down the sides a few times, until fully combined and the mixture forms a thick paste.

2. Cut the steaks into portions that will fit in your grill pan and are of even thickness. Lay the steaks on a baking sheet and slather on both sides with the herb paste. Cover with plastic wrap and let sit at room temperature for 30 minutes.

3. Trim the rest of the green onions and drizzle with a little oil. Toss to make sure the onions are coated with a light layer of oil.

4. Place a cast-iron grill pan over high heat and preheat for 5 minutes.

5. Pat the steaks dry with paper towels leaving some of the herbs on the steak. Grill for 3 to 4 minutes per side, depending on thickness. Remove from grill pan and let rest for at least 5 minutes before slicing. Finish cooking the rest of the steak portions.

6. Put the green onions in the grill pan and cook about 2 minutes per side. Remove from grill pan and serve with sliced steak, tortillas, salsa, avocado and lime wedges.

Duke in *Chisum* (1970).

RIO LOBO RIBEYE

Like a classic John Wayne Western, this steak is sure to please every time.

PROVISIONS

1 (1½-in. thick) ribeye steak, about 1¼ lb.

Vegetable oil

Kosher or fine sea salt, to taste

Pepper, to taste

Cayenne pepper, to taste

1 Tbsp. butter, softened

DIRECTIONS

1. Place a cast-iron skillet in the oven and heat to 500 degrees F. Bring the steak to room temperature. Place a wire cooling rack over a sheet pan.

2. When the oven reaches temperature, carefully remove the skillet and place on a burner over high heat. Heat the skillet for 5 minutes. Leave the oven on.

3. Pat steak dry with paper towels. Coat the steak with oil and season generously with salt, pepper, and cayenne pepper on both sides.

4. Place the steak in the hot skillet and cook, undisturbed for 1 minute. Flip and cook for another 30 seconds. Place the skillet in the oven, cook for 3 minutes, flip and cook for another 3 minutes or until internal temperature reaches 120 to 125 degrees F for medium-rare. Add another minute per side for an internal temperature of 130 degrees F for medium. Remove the steak from the pan, place on wire rack and spread the butter on top. Cover loosely with foil and let sit for 5 minutes before serving. Serve whole or sliced.

Duke in *Rio Lobo* (1970).

DID YOU KNOW?

Famed stuntman and friend of Duke Yakima Canutt served as a second unit director on *Rio Lobo*.

FREEDOM FAJITAS

Pursue your culinary happiness by cooking up these lip-smackin' fajitas.

SERVES 6

PROVISIONS

STEAK

- ½ **cup olive oil**
- ½ **cup orange juice**
- **Juice of 2 limes**
- 1 **jalapeño pepper, seeded, deveined and minced**
- 3 **garlic cloves, minced**
- 1 **tsp. dried cumin**
- 1 **tsp. dried oregano**
- 1 **tsp. salt**
- ½ **tsp. pepper**
- 1 **lb. flank steak**

VEGETABLES

- 1 **large white or yellow onion, cut in half and thinly sliced**
- 1 **red bell pepper, seeded, deveined and thinly sliced**
- 1 **yellow bell pepper, seeded, deveined and thinly sliced**
- 2 **cubanelle peppers (or 1 green bell pepper), seeded, deveined and thinly sliced**
- 2 **Tbsp. olive oil**
- **Juice of 1 lime**

FOR SERVING

- **Corn or flour tortillas, warmed**
- **Salsa**
- **Grated cheese**
- **Guacamole**
- **Lime wedges**

DIRECTIONS

1. Whisk together the olive oil, orange juice, lime juice, jalapeño pepper, garlic, cumin, oregano, salt and pepper, and pour into a large food storage bag. Add the flank steak, turn over a few times to coat and refrigerate for 4 to 8 hours. Remove the steak from the marinade, discarding the marinade, pat dry and let come to room temperature.

2. Combine all the vegetable ingredients in a large mixing bowl and let sit while the steak is cooking.

3. Heat a cast-iron grill pan over medium-high for 5 minutes. Spray with cooking spray, add the steak and cook, undisturbed, for 4 minutes. Flip and cook for another 4 to 5 minutes or until it reaches desired degree of doneness. Let steak rest for 10 minutes before slicing thinly across the grain.

4. While the steak is resting, cook the vegetables. Wipe out the cast-iron grill pan, place back on stove over high heat and, using tongs, add the vegetables to the hot grill pan. Cook, turning occasionally, until tender and starting to brown, about 8 minutes.

5. Serve the steak and vegetables with tortillas, salsa, grated cheese, guacamole and lime wedges, and let everyone make their own fajitas.

John Wayne and others in a scene from *The Night Riders* (1939).

John Wayne in *Rio Grande* (1950). The film was the last entry in director John Ford's Cavalry Trilogy, which also consists of *Fort Apache* (1948), *She Wore a Yellow Ribbon* (1949) and *Rio Grande*.

SHEPHERD OF THE HILLS PIE

This dish is every bit as hearty as John Wayne's classic character Young Matt Matthews.

SERVES 6 TO 8

PROVISIONS

- 2 lb. Idaho potatoes, peeled and diced
- 6 Tbsp. butter
- ½ cup milk
- Kosher or fine sea salt, to taste
- Pepper, to taste
- 1 Tbsp. olive oil
- 2 large carrots, peeled and diced
- 1 large white or yellow onion, diced
- 8 oz. white mushrooms, tough ends of stem removed and cut into large dice
- 1 lb. ground chuck
- 3 Tbsp. steak sauce
- 1 cup beef broth
- 1 cup frozen peas
- 1½ cups grated Monterey Jack cheese
- ½ cup grated Parmesan cheese

DIRECTIONS

1. Preheat oven to 375 degrees F.

2. Bring the potatoes to a boil in salted water. Cook until tender, about 20 minutes. Mash with butter and milk. Season to taste with salt and pepper. Set aside.

3. While the potatoes are boiling, start the filling. Heat the oil in a 12-in. cast-iron skillet over medium-high. Add the carrots and onions and cook, stirring occasionally, until they start to soften, about 5 minutes. Add the mushrooms and cook, stirring occasionally, for another 5 minutes. Add the ground chuck and cook, breaking it up, until no longer pink. Push the mixture to one side of the skillet and sop up the excess oil with paper towels. Add the steak sauce and cook, stirring, for 1 minute.

4. Add the beef broth and simmer for 10 minutes. Stir in the peas. Spread the potatoes on top of the filling and smooth into an even layer making sure the potatoes reach the edges of the skillet. Make a cross hatch pattern with a fork on top of the potatoes and bake for 30 minutes. Turn on the broiler, combine the cheeses and sprinkle evenly over the top of the shepherd's pie. Broil until the cheeses are melted and the top is golden, about 3 minutes.

Betty Field and John Wayne in *The Shepherd of the Hills* (1941).

DID YOU KNOW?

The Shepherd of the Hills was the first movie John Wayne appeared in that was filmed in Technicolor, the dominant process for film coloring until the mid 1950s.

SKIRT STEAK WITH BLISTERED CORN SALSA

Don't skirt around the issue of hunger, pilgrim—
attack it head on with a helping of this Duke-worthy dish.

SERVES 6 TO 8

PROVISIONS

- 4 Tbsp. olive oil
- Juice of 2 limes, divided
- 1 large jalapeño pepper, seeded, deveined and minced, divided
- 1½ tsp. kosher or fine sea salt, plus more to taste
- ¾ tsp. pepper, plus more to taste
- 1 Tbsp. chili powder
- 1 tsp. ground cumin
- 1 (2- to 2 ½-lb.) skirt steak
- 1½ cups fresh or frozen and thawed corn kernels
- 3 plum or roma tomatoes, seeded and chopped
- ½ small red onion, finely chopped
- ½ cup fresh cilantro, chopped

DIRECTIONS

1. Combine the olive oil, juice of 1 lime, half the minced jalapeño pepper, 1½ tsp. salt, ¾ tsp. pepper and the cumin in a mixing bowl and whisk to combine. Pour into a plastic food storage bag. Cut the skirt steak into pieces that will fit into a cast-iron skillet and are of even thickness. Add to the bag, toss to coat and let sit at room temperature for 30 minutes.

2. Heat a large cast-iron skillet over high for 3 minutes. Add the corn and cook, stirring occasionally, until browned in spots and warm. Place in a bowl with the juice of 1 lime, the remaining jalapeño pepper, chopped tomatoes, onion and cilantro. Stir and let sit at room temperature while cooking the steak.

3. Heat the cast-iron skillet over medium high for 3 minutes. Pat the steak dry, discard the marinade and add the steak, in batches, to the pan and cook 3 to 4 minutes per side, depending on thickness. Remove from pan and let sit at least 5 minutes. Finish cooking the rest of the steak in the same manner.

4. Taste the corn salsa, add salt and pepper if needed. Slice the steak and place on a bed of the corn salsa.

John Wayne in *The Comancheros* (1961).

SLOPPY JAKES

When your appetite's the size of Big Jake McCandles, knock it down with one of these sandwiches.

SERVES 4 TO 6

PROVISIONS

- 1¼ lb. ground chuck
- ¼ cup brown sugar
- 1 tsp. garlic powder
- 1 tsp. onion powder
- 1½ tsp. kosher or fine sea salt
- 1 tsp. pepper
- ¼ tsp. red pepper flakes
- 1 medium white or yellow onion, diced
- 1 green bell pepper, seeded, deveined and diced
- 1 Tbsp. Worcestershire sauce
- 2 Tbsp. tomato paste
- 2 cups tomato puree or sauce
- 4–6 crusty rolls, split, toasted and lightly buttered

DIRECTIONS

1. Heat a cast-iron skillet over medium-high for 3 minutes. Add the ground chuck and cook, breaking it up, until no longer pink. Drain off any excess fat. Add the brown sugar and spices. Cook for 1 minute, stirring. Add the onion, bell pepper and Worcestershire sauce, reduce heat to medium and cook, stirring occasionally, until the vegetables are tender, about 5 minutes. Add the tomato paste and cook, stirring, for 1 minute. Add the tomato puree or sauce, stir to combine, bring to a simmer and let simmer for 5 to 10 minutes. Pile the mixture onto buns and serve.

DID YOU KNOW?

Big Jake was the last of five movies John Wayne and Maureen O'Hara starred in together, a series of films beginning with John Ford's *Rio Grande* in 1950.

John Wayne and Maureen O'Hara in *Big Jake* (1971).

103

BACON-WRAPPED FILET MIGNON

A steak wrapped in bacon? That's a meal John Wayne would saddle up for.

SERVES 4

PROVISIONS

- 4 filets, about 8 oz. each
- 4 slices bacon
- Kosher or fine sea salt, to taste
- Pepper, to taste
- 1 Tbsp. vegetable oil
- 1 Tbsp. butter

DIRECTIONS

1. Preheat oven to 450 degrees F. Wrap a piece of bacon around each steak, securing with a toothpick. Let come to room temperature. Season generously with salt and pepper on both sides.

2. Heat a cast-iron skillet over high for 3 minutes. Add the oil and butter and heat until the butter melts. Add the steaks, cook for 1 minute without moving, flip, cook for another 30 seconds, then place the skillet in the oven for 7 to 10 minutes or until the internal temperature of the steaks is 120 to 125 degrees F for medium rare. Let sit for 5 minutes before serving.

Duke in *Cahill U.S. Marshal* (1973).

104

BLT BURGER

Sometimes, it's the simple things in life that give us the most pleasure.
And it doesn't get simpler than bacon, lettuce, tomato and beef.

SERVES 6

PROVISIONS

SAUCE

- ¾ cup mayonnaise
- ¼ cup ketchup
- 2 Tbsp. sweet chili sauce
- 2 Tbsp. pickle relish
- 2 Tbsp. very finely minced white onion
- 1 Tbsp. Worcestershire sauce

BURGERS

- 6 slices thick cut bacon, cut in half crosswise
- 2 lb. ground chuck
- Kosher or fine sea salt, to taste
- Pepper, to taste
- 6 Kaiser rolls or hamburger buns
- Lettuce leaves
- Thick slices of tomato

DIRECTIONS

SAUCE

1. Combine all ingredients in a mixing bowl and mix well. Cover with plastic wrap and refrigerate until serving time.

BURGERS

1. Place the bacon in a cold cast-iron skillet, turn the heat to medium, and cook the bacon until crispy, turning occasionally. Let drain on paper towels.

2. Divide the ground chuck into 6 equal-sized portions. Loosely form each portion into a patty ¾-in. thick. Make a deep impression in the center of each patty and season generously with salt and pepper on both sides.

3. Remove all but 3 Tbsp. of bacon fat and turn the heat to medium-high. Add the patties and cook until the burgers are golden brown and slightly charred, about 3 minutes. Flip the burgers and cook for 4 minutes (for medium-rare) or until golden brown and slightly charred.

4. Spread sauce on both sides of the burger buns, put lettuce on the bottom bun, top with tomato, burger patty and bacon.

John Wayne and a cheetah in *Hatari!* (1962).

DID YOU KNOW?

The word "hatari" means "danger" in Swahili, but the film's actors managed to make it through the shoot without suffering serious harm, despite working with live anim...

OVEN-BAKED PORK CHOPS AND BAKED BEANS

A plate full of chops and baked beans means someone's about to tuck into a satisfying dinner.

SERVES 8

PROVISIONS

Vegetable oil

8 bone-in pork chops

Kosher or fine sea salt, to taste

Pepper, to taste

3 (1 lb.) cans baked beans or 6 cups Bacony Baked Beans (see recipe on page 41)

1 medium white or yellow onion, diced

1 green bell pepper, seeded, deveined and diced

3 garlic cloves, minced

¼ cup ketchup

¼ cup brown sugar, packed

2 Tbsp. Dijon mustard

DIRECTIONS

1. Preheat oven to 350 degrees F.

2. Pour enough oil in the bottom of a large skillet to coat the bottom and heat it over medium-high. Season the pork chops with salt and pepper on both sides. Brown the pork chops, in batches, on both sides, about 4 minutes per side. Remove the chops from the skillet.

3. In a large mixing bowl, combine the beans, onion, green pepper, garlic, ketchup, brown sugar and mustard. Spoon some of the beans into a cast-iron Dutch oven. Put enough pork chops to fit in an even layer. Add more beans and continue layering, ending with beans. Bake, covered, for 30 minutes. Remove the cover and continue to bake for another 30 to 40 minutes or until the chops are tender.

Duke and Henry Fonda face off in *Fort Apache* (1948).

BRINED PORK CHOPS

These mouth-watering chops have the ability to turn a mediocre night into a great one.

SERVES 4

PROVISIONS

BRINED PORK CHOPS

- 4 cups water, divided
- ¼ cup kosher salt
- ¼ cup brown sugar, packed
- 1 tsp. black pepper
- 1 Tbsp. apple cider vinegar
- 4 pork chops about ¾-in. thick
- ½ white onion, sliced
- 2–3 sprigs fresh sage
- Olive oil for brushing the pork chops

SPICY PEAR CHUTNEY

- 1 Tbsp. olive oil
- ½ medium sized red onion, minced
- ½ cup dried cranberries
- ¼ cup sugar
- 1 Tbsp. apple cider vinegar
- 1 Tbsp. freshly squeezed lemon juice
- 1 tsp. kosher or fine sea salt
- ½ tsp. black pepper
- ¼–½ tsp. red pepper flakes (depending on how spicy you want it)
- 3 fresh pears, cored and chopped

DIRECTIONS

BRINED PORK CHOPS

1. Combine 1 cup water with the salt, brown sugar and pepper in a small saucepan. Heat, stirring until the salt and sugar dissolve. Add 3 cups of cold water and let the mixture cool. Stir in the apple cider vinegar. Pour mixture into a glass baking dish or large plastic storage bag. Add the pork chops, onions and sage. Refrigerate for 1 to 12 hours. Even a little bit of brining is better than none.

2. Take pork chops out of the fridge and rinse them well with cold water, then pat dry with paper towels. Let set for about 5 minutes before cooking.

3. Heat a cast-iron grill pan or skillet over medium high. Brush the pork chops with olive oil and cook for 4 minutes per side (more or less depending on the thickness of the pork chops). Remove from pan, brush the top with a little more olive oil and let rest for 5 minutes before serving with spicy pear chutney.

SPICY PEAR CHUTNEY

1. Heat a large saucepan over medium. Add the olive oil and minced red onion. Cook for 2 or 3 minutes until the onions start to soften. Add the dried cranberries and cook for 5 more minutes. Stir in the sugar, vinegar, lemon juice, salt, pepper, red pepper flakes and pears. Combine well. Simmer on low heat for 5 to 10 minutes or until the pears and cranberries have softened but the pears still retain their shape. If the mixture is too wet, turn the heat up and cook until most of the liquid has evaporated. Serve warm.

John Wayne in *Island in the Sky* (1953).

BARBECUE PORK BURGERS WITH COLESLAW

These burgers pack in a whole barbecue's worth of taste between two buns.

SERVES 4

PROVISIONS

- ¼ cup mayonnaise
- 1 Tbsp. milk
- 2 tsp. sugar
- 1½ tsp. white vinegar
- 2½ cups packaged coleslaw mix
- Kosher or fine sea salt, to taste
- Pepper, to taste
- 1½ lb. ground pork
- 4 Tbsp. barbecue sauce, divided, plus more for serving if desired
- 2 Tbsp. vegetable oil
- 4 hamburger buns

DIRECTIONS

1. Place a cast-iron skillet in the oven and heat to 500 degrees F.

2. Combine the mayonnaise, milk, sugar and vinegar in a mixing bowl. Add the coleslaw mix and toss to coat. Season to taste with salt and pepper. Let sit at room temperature while making the burgers.

3. Combine the pork with 1 tsp. salt, ½ tsp. pepper and 3 Tbsp. barbecue sauce. Divide the mixture into 4 equal-sized portions. Loosely form each portion into a patty ¾-in. thick. Make a deep impression in the center of each patty. Place in the refrigerator while the oven heats up.

4. When the oven reaches 500 degrees F, carefully remove the skillet and place on the stove over medium-high heat and turn off the oven.

5. Add the oil to the pan and heat until it shimmers. Add the patties and cook until the burgers are golden brown and slightly charred, about 4 minutes. Flip the burgers and cook for 3 to 4 minutes or until the burgers are cooked through. Brush the cooked burgers with barbecue sauce.

6. Serve on buns with coleslaw and more barbecue sauce on the side if desired.

John Wayne from *In Old Oklahoma* (1943).

PAN-FRIED PORK CHOPS

There's nothing easier than throwing some chops in a skillet. Nothing tastier, either.

MAKES 8 PORK CHOPS

PROVISIONS

- 8   thin-cut bone-in pork chops
- 1   cup flour
- 1   tsp. kosher or fine sea salt
- 1   tsp. pepper
- 1   tsp. garlic powder
- 1   tsp. paprika
- ½   cup vegetable oil
- 2   Tbsp. butter

DIRECTIONS

1. Dry the pork chops well with paper towels. Combine the flour, salt, pepper, garlic powder and paprika on a plate and mix well. Dredge the pork chops in the flour mixture and place on a clean plate. Let sit for 2 to 3 minutes then dredge them in the flour mixture again.

2. Heat the oil in a large cast-iron skillet over medium-high. Add the butter and let it melt. Fry the pork chops 2 to 3 at a time for 3 to 4 minutes or until golden brown. Flip and fry on the other side for 2 minutes or until golden brown and no pink juices remain. Keep warm while frying the rest of the pork chops.

Rock Hudson and John Wayne in *The Undefeated* (1969).

DID YOU KNOW?

John Wayne and Rock Hudson would often pass the time on set in between takes with one of Duke's favorite activities—playing chess!

BACON-WRAPPED PORK TENDERLOIN

Go ahead and pig out on this meal. You've earned it.

SERVES 4

PROVISIONS

- 8 slices regular (not thick cut) bacon
- 1 (1–1½ lb.) pork tenderloin
- Pepper, to taste
- 1 Tbsp. olive oil
- 2 Tbsp. honey

DIRECTIONS

1. Place a cast-iron skillet in the oven and preheat oven to 350 degrees F.

2. Cut the bacon in half crosswise and lay the pieces next to each other on a cutting board, slightly overlapping each other. Sprinkle the pork tenderloin with a little pepper all over and lay on top of the bacon slices. Fold the bacon up over the pork, securing with toothpicks if needed.

3. Carefully remove the skillet from the oven, place the oil in the pan and swirl the pan to coat the bottom. Place the pork in the skillet, brush with the honey and bake for 30 minutes or until the pork reaches an internal temperature of 140 degrees F, basting with the pan juices occasionally. Turn on the broiler and broil until the bacon on top is crisp, about 2 to 3 minutes. Baste the tenderloin again with the pan juice, cover loosely with foil and let rest 5 minutes before slicing and serving.

John Wayne in *The Big Trail* (1930).

John Wayne in
*The Sons of Katie
Elder* (1965).
As a child, John
Wayne would
ride to school on
a pony named
Jenny.

PAN-FRIED PORK CHOPS WITH COUNTRY GRAVY

This dinner delivers good old-fashioned flavor, just like you had as a young'un.

SERVES 4 TO 6

PROVISIONS

- 8 thin-cut bone-in pork chops
- 1½ cups flour
- 1½ tsp. kosher or fine sea salt, plus more to taste
- 1 tsp. pepper, plus more to taste
- 1½ tsp. paprika
- 4 Tbsp. olive oil
- 7 Tbsp. butter, divided
- 2¼ cups milk

DIRECTIONS

1. Dry the pork chops well with paper towels. Combine the flour, 1½ tsp. salt, 1 tsp. pepper and paprika on a plate and mix well. Dredge the pork chops in the flour mixture and place on a clean plate. Let sit for 2 to 3 minutes then dredge them in the flour mixture again. Save 3 Tbsp. of the flour mixture.

2. Heat the oil in a large cast-iron skillet over medium-high. Add the butter and let it melt. Fry the pork chops in batches until well browned, about 2 to 3 minutes per side. Remove to a plate and keep warm.

3. Add 3 Tbsp. butter to the pan along with the reserved 3 Tbsp. of flour. Whisk until smooth and cook for 1 minute, whisking constantly. Add the milk and cook, whisking, until the gravy thickens, about 4 minutes. Taste and add more salt and pepper if needed. Serve the pork chops covered with the gravy.

DID YOU KNOW?

Although John Wayne had worked as a bit actor and propman with mentor John Ford early in his career, *Stagecoach* was the first time Ford cast Duke in a major role.

Claire Trevor and John Wayne in *Stagecoach* (1939).

SMOTHERED PORK CHOPS

Serve this classic dish the way it was meant to be—covered in gravy.

SERVES 4 TO 6

PROVISIONS

- 8   thin-cut bone-in pork chops
- 1½ cups flour
- 1½ tsp. kosher or fine sea salt, plus more to taste
- 1   tsp. pepper, plus more to taste
- 1½ tsp. garlic powder
- 1½ tsp. paprika
- ¼ tsp. cayenne pepper
- 4   Tbsp. olive oil
- 7   Tbsp. butter, use divided
- 1   large white or yellow onion, thinly sliced
- 1   red bell pepper, seeded, deveined and thinly sliced
- 1   yellow bell pepper, seeded, deveined and thinly sliced
- 1   green bell pepper, seeded, deveined and thinly sliced
- 2   cups chicken broth
- 1   Tbsp. Worcestershire sauce
- 2   Tbsp. heavy cream

DIRECTIONS

1. Dry the pork chops well with paper towels. Combine the flour, 1½ tsp. salt, 1 tsp. pepper, garlic powder, paprika and cayenne pepper on a plate and mix well. Dredge the pork chops in the flour mixture and place on a clean plate. Let sit for 2 to 3 minutes then dredge them in the flour mixture again. Save 3 Tbsp. of the flour mixture.

2. Heat the oil in a large cast-iron skillet over medium-high. Add the butter and let it melt. Fry the pork chops in batches until well browned, about 2 to 3 minutes per side. Remove to a plate and keep warm. Add the onion and peppers to the same pan and cook, stirring occasionally, until softened and starting to brown, about 8 minutes. Remove to a plate.

3. Add 3 Tbsp. butter to the pan along with the reserved 3 Tbsp. of flour. Whisk until smooth and cook for 1 minute, whisking constantly. Add the chicken broth and Worcestershire sauce and cook, whisking, until the gravy thickens, about 4 minutes. Whisk in the heavy cream. Taste and add more salt and pepper if needed. Stir in the vegetables, coating them with sauce. Serve the pork chops covered with the gravy.

John Wayne and Walter Brennan in *Dakota* (1945).

SAUSAGE AND PEPPER SANDWICHES

Tell your kin to grab a roll and get in line—these sandwiches are a hot item!

SERVES 6

PROVISIONS

- 6 sweet or hot Italian sausages
- 1 Tbsp. olive oil
- 1 Tbsp. butter
- 1 medium white or yellow onion, thinly sliced
- 1 red bell pepper, seeded, deveined and thinly sliced
- 1 green bell pepper, seeded, deveined and thinly sliced
- 4 garlic cloves, minced
- 2 tsp. Italian seasoning
- 1 tsp. kosher or fine sea salt
- ½ tsp. pepper
- 6 hoagie rolls

DIRECTIONS

1. Place the sausages in a large cast-iron skillet over medium heat and brown on all sides. Remove from the pan.

2. Add the oil and butter to the pan and heat until the butter melts. Add the onions and peppers and cook, stirring occasionally, for 2 to 3 minutes. Add the garlic and Italian seasoning, salt and pepper, and cook, stirring, for 30 seconds. Add the sausages back to the pan, turn the heat to low, cover with a lid or another skillet and cook until the pepper and onions are tender and the sausages are heated through, 10 to 15 minutes.

3. Serve the sausages on hoagie rolls with peppers and onions piled on.

John Wayne takes a stroll through the streets of Rome, Italy.

DID YOU KNOW?

For his 1957 film *Legend of the Lost*, Duke collaborated with international star Sophia Loren and shot the film in Rome.

SEA CHASE SAUERKRAUT BRAISED BRATWURST

Serve up these delicious links and you'll be the captain of the cookout.

SERVES 6

PROVISIONS

- 2 Tbsp. vegetable oil
- 6 fresh bratwurst links
- 2 lb. red potatoes, scrubbed, unpeeled and cut into large chunks
- 1 large white or yellow onion, diced
- 3 garlic cloves, minced
- 2 Tbsp. brown sugar
- 1 lb. sauerkraut, drained
- 3 cups chicken broth
- 2 tsp. caraway seeds

DIRECTIONS

1. Heat the oil in a large cast-iron skillet over medium-high. Prick holes in the casing of the bratwurst and add to the hot pan, brown well on all sides. Remove the sausages to a plate, add the potatoes and onions and cook, stirring occasionally, until they start to brown, about 5 minutes. Add the garlic and cook for 30 seconds, stirring. Add the brown sugar, stir to combine, then add the sauerkraut, chicken broth and caraway seeds. Bring to a simmer, reduce heat and simmer for 45 minutes.

Duke and Lana Turner in *The Sea Chase* (1955).

BRAISED CHICKEN THIGHS WITH ROOT VEGETABLES

This back-to-basics meal may surprise you with how quickly it becomes your new favorite.

SERVES 4 TO 6

PROVISIONS

- 2 tsp. paprika
- 1 tsp. garlic powder
- 1½ tsp. kosher or fine sea salt, plus more to taste
- ¾ tsp. pepper, plus more to taste
- 6 boneless, skinless chicken thighs, trimmed of excess fat
- 2 Tbsp. olive oil
- 1 large red onion, diced
- ⅓ cup apple cider
- 1 lb. baby red potatoes, scrubbed and cut in half
- ½ lb. baby carrots
- 2 Tbsp. flour
- 1½ cups chicken broth
- 4 thyme sprigs, plus more for garnish

DIRECTIONS

1. Combine the paprika, garlic powder, 1½ tsp. salt and ¾ tsp. pepper in a small bowl. Coat the chicken thighs with the spice mixture.

2. Heat a cast-iron Dutch oven over medium-high for 3 minutes. Add the oil and let heat for a minute. Add the chicken thighs, in batches, and brown on both sides, about 4 to 5 minutes per side. Remove the chicken to a plate.

3. Add the onion and cook, stirring occasionally, until they begin to soften, about 5 minutes. Add the cider and cook stirring, until it is almost all evaporated. Add the potatoes, carrots and flour. Season with a large pinch of salt and pepper. Stir to coat the vegetables with the flour and cook for 1 minute. Gradually stir in the broth and bring to a boil, stirring frequently. Add the chicken along with any juices that have accumulated back to the pan. Add the thyme springs. Reduce heat to medium-low, cover the pan and let simmer until the chicken is cooked through and the vegetables are tender, about 25 minutes. Turn the chicken occasionally while it cooks. Taste and adjust seasoning with more salt and pepper if needed. Garnish with fresh thyme if desired.

DID YOU KNOW?

The director of *Legend of the Lost*, Henry Hathaway, also directed Duke in several films, including *True Grit* (1969).

Duke in *Legend of the Lost* (1957).

CHICKEN FRIED STEAK

For the times you want to add a little crunch to your steak, reach for this recipe.

SERVES 4

PROVISIONS

- 1 **cup flour**
- 1 **tsp. kosher or fine sea salt, plus more to taste**
- 1 **tsp. pepper, plus more to taste**
- 1 **tsp. paprika**
- 3 **large eggs**
- 2½ **cups milk, divided**
- 4 **pieces (8 oz. each) cube steak**
  Vegetable oil
- ½ **cup chicken broth**
  Mashed potatoes, for serving

Yakima Canutt and John Wayne in *King of the Pecos* (1936).

DIRECTIONS

1. Preheat oven to 200 degrees F. Place a wire cooling rack over a rimmed baking sheet.

2. Line up 3 pie plates or shallow bowls. In one, mix the flour with 1 tsp. salt, 1 tsp. pepper and the paprika. Put the eggs in another bowl and lightly beat with a fork. Place ½ cup milk in the last bowl. Lightly season the cube steaks with salt and pepper on both sides.

3. Dip the steaks into the milk, then into the flour, then the eggs and finally back in the flour. Place on a plate and let sit for 10 to 15 minutes. Reserve the flour mixture.

4. Pour enough oil into a large cast-iron skillet to coat the bottom with about ⅛ inch of oil. Heat the oil over medium-high until it shimmers. Fry the steaks in batches until golden brown on both sides, about 4 minutes per side. Place the steaks on the wire rack over the sheet pan and keep warm in the oven.

5. When the steaks are done, remove all but 3 Tbsp. oil. Add 3 Tbsp. of the reserved flour mixture to the oil and whisk. Continue to cook, whisking, for 1 minute. Add the chicken broth and remaining 2 cups milk. Cook, whisking frequently, until the gravy thickens, about 5 minutes. Season to taste with salt and plenty of pepper.

6. Serve the steaks with mashed potatoes covered with gravy.

SKILLET CHICKEN POT PIE

A new spin on an old favorite.

SERVES 6

PROVISIONS

- 1 premade piecrust
- 1 egg
- 4 Tbsp. butter
- 1 medium white or yellow onion, diced
- 2 medium carrots, peeled and diced
- 3 Tbsp. flour
- 1½ cups chicken broth
- 1½ cups milk
- 3 cups chopped cooked chicken
- 1½ cups frozen peas
-    Kosher or fine sea salt, to taste
-    Pepper, to taste

DIRECTIONS

1. Roll the crust between two pieces of parchment paper to about 1 in. larger than the top of your cast-iron skillet. Remove the top piece of parchment paper. Fold in the outer ½ in. of the dough and crimp to make an attractive border. Cut 4 slits in the center. Place the crust with the parchment paper on a baking sheet and refrigerate for 15 minutes.

2. Preheat oven to 400 degrees F.

3. Remove the crust from the refrigerator, whisk egg with 1 Tbsp. water and brush over the top of the crust. Bake until golden brown, 12 to 15 minutes. Remove from oven but leave oven on.

4. Melt the butter over medium heat in a cast-iron skillet. Add the onions and carrots and cook, stirring occasionally, until the onions soften, about 5 minutes. Add the flour and cook, stirring, for 1 minute. Add the chicken broth and milk and cook, stirring occasionally, until the sauce thickens, about 8 minutes. Stir in the chicken and peas, taste and season to taste with salt and pepper. Top with the parbaked crust and bake until the crust is deeply golden brown and the filling is bubbly, 10 to 15 minutes.

John Wayne in
The Quiet Man
(1952).

DID YOU KNOW?

John Wayne's paternal family emigrated to the United States from Ireland—which is the setting of *The Quiet Man!*

THE FIGHTING KENTUCKIAN'S FRIED CHICKEN

This crispy chicken is worth fighting for (but luckily, you don't have to!).

SERVES 4 TO 5

PROVISIONS

- 3 **cups buttermilk**
- **Kosher or fine sea salt, to taste**
- 1 **Tbsp. hot sauce**
- 1 **whole fryer chicken, cut into 10 pieces**
- 2 **cups flour**
- 2 **Tbsp. paprika**
- 1 **Tbsp. garlic powder**
- 1 **Tbsp. onion powder**
- **Pepper, to taste**
- **Vegetable shortening**

DIRECTIONS

1. Start this recipe the night before or early in the day you plan to serve the chicken. An instant read thermometer is useful not only for keeping the oil temperature correct but also for checking the doneness of the chicken.

2. In a large mixing bowl large enough to hold all the chicken, combine the buttermilk with 1 Tbsp. salt and the hot sauce. Add the chicken, stir to coat, cover the bowl with plastic wrap and refrigerate 8 to 24 hours.

3. Drain the chicken in a colander.

4. In a large paper bag, combine the flour, paprika, garlic powder, onion powder, 2 tsp. salt and 2 tsp. pepper. Shake to mix.

5. Add chicken (do not dry off buttermilk) to the bag, a few pieces at a time, and shake vigorously to coat. Place chicken on a board or plate and let sit while the shortening melts and heats.

6. Place a wire cooling rack over a sheet pan.

7. Put a large cast-iron skillet on the stove over low heat. Add enough vegetable shortening to come up ½ in. on the skillet. Let the shortening melt then raise the heat to medium and heat the oil to 325 degrees F. Fry the chicken in batches, making sure not to cover or crowd the pan. Fry until golden brown on both sides and the chicken has an internal temperature of 165 degrees F, 7 to 12 minutes per side depending on size. As the chicken pieces get done, place them on the wire rack to drain and sprinkle with a pinch of salt while still hot. Make sure the shortening temperature does not go above 325 degrees F or below 300 degrees F. Keep adjusting the heat as needed.

Duke in *The Fighting Kentuckian* (1949).

WAYNE FAMILY
═ TIP ═

When the chicken is finished, be
sure to avoid the urge to soak
up the grease with paper towels.
This can actually make the nice
crispy finish turn soggy—and no
one wants that!

FINGER-LICKIN' BBQ CHICKEN

Pick this recipe when you don't feel like doing the dishes. The plates are guaranteed to be licked clean!

SERVES 4 TO 6

PROVISIONS

- 1 Tbsp. vegetable oil
- 1 Tbsp. brown sugar
- 1 Tbsp. chili powder
- 1 tsp. onion powder
- 1 tsp. garlic powder
- 1 tsp. kosher or fine sea salt
- ½ tsp. pepper
- 3 lb. bone-in, skin-on chicken thighs and drumsticks
- 1 small white or yellow onion, very finely diced
- ⅔ cup ketchup
- ⅓ cup water
- 1 Tbsp. Worcestershire sauce
- 1 Tbsp. apple cider vinegar
- ½ tsp. dry mustard powder

DIRECTIONS

1. Place a 12-in. cast-iron skillet in the oven and preheat to 500 degrees F.

2. Combine the oil with the brown sugar, chili powder, onion powder, garlic powder, salt and pepper. Pat the chicken pieces dry and rub the pieces all over with the spice mixture.

3. When the oven comes to temperature, place the chicken, skin side down, in the skillet, and reduce the oven temperature to 450 degrees F. Roast the chicken until well browned, turning once halfway through, about 25 to 30 minutes total. Carefully remove the skillet, transfer the chicken to a serving platter and let rest while making the sauce.

4. Pour off all but 1 Tbsp. of the oil from the skillet. Place on the stove over medium heat. Add the onions and cook, stirring occasionally, until softened, about 5 minutes. Add the ketchup, water, Worcestershire sauce, vinegar and dry mustard, and stir well. Cook, stirring occasionally, until the sauce has reduced to about 1 cup, about 5 minutes. Stir in any juices that have accumulated from the chicken. Take the skillet off the heat. Add the chicken, toss to coat well and remove the chicken back to a serving platter. Serve any additional sauce on the side.

John Wayne in *Haunted Gold* (1932).

DID YOU KNOW?

John Wayne made dozens of B-movies between 1930 and 1939 for a variety of studios that were collectively known as "Poverty Row."

HONDO'S ROASTED CHICKEN

Whether you're a dispatch rider or a hungry ranch hand, this big bird is sure to satisfy.

SERVES 4 TO 6

PROVISIONS

- 1 (3½–4 lb.) whole chicken, giblets removed, rinsed and patted dry
- 4 Tbsp. butter, softened

  Kosher or fine sea salt, to taste

  Pepper, to taste
- 2 whole lemons, quartered
- 3 sprigs rosemary
- 1 large white yellow onion, sliced

DIRECTIONS

1. Preheat oven to 450 degrees F.

2. Sprinkle the cavity of the chicken with salt and pepper. Stuff the lemon wedges and rosemary sprigs inside. Tie the chicken legs together with string. Rub the butter over the chicken, season with salt and pepper. Layer the onion slices on the bottom of a cast iron Dutch oven. Place the chicken on top of the onion slices. Roast for 45 minutes or until the juices run clear.

3. Let sit for 10 minutes. Untie the legs, remove the lemons and rosemary, and serve.

John Wayne and Geraldine Page in *Hondo* (1953).

SKILLET CHICKEN PARMESAN

Give this Old Country staple some new western sizzle—your guests will be glad you did.

SERVES 4

PROVISIONS

- 2 **boneless, skinless chicken breasts**
- 2 **large eggs**
- ½ **tsp. kosher or fine sea salt, plus more to taste**
- ½ **tsp. freshly ground black pepper, plus more to taste**
- 1 **cup panko style breadcrumbs**
- ¼ **cup grated Parmesan cheese, plus more for serving**
- 1½ **tsp. Italian seasoning, divided**
- 1 **tsp. garlic powder**
- 4 **Tbsp. olive oil, divided**
- 2 **Tbsp. butter, divided**
- ½ **cup marinara sauce**
- 4 **oz. fresh mozzarella cheese, grated**
- 8 **basil leaves, thinly sliced**

DIRECTIONS

1. Place the chicken breasts on a cutting board, place one hand on top and, with a sharp knife parallel to the cutting board, cut the breasts in half widthwise all the way through to create 2 halves of equal size per breast. Place each of the 4 breast halves between two pieces of plastic wrap and pound them out thinly with a rolling pin.

2. On a plate, combine the eggs with a large pinch of salt and pepper and whisk.

3. On another plate, combine the breadcrumbs, Parmesan cheese, Italian seasoning, garlic powder, ½ tsp. salt and ½ tsp. pepper.

4. Dip the chicken breast halves into the egg first then coat with the breadcrumb mixture, pressing the mixture onto the chicken breasts.

5. Position the top rack of the oven about 6 in. from the top and preheat the broiler to high. Line a baking sheet with parchment paper or a silicone baking mat.

6. In a large cast-iron skillet, heat 2 Tbsp. olive oil until hot over medium-high. Add 1 Tbsp. butter and once melted, add 2 of the coated chicken breast pieces. Fry for about 4 minutes per side or until golden brown. Place on prepared baking pan. Add another 2 Tbsp. of oil to the pan, let it heat up, add the remaining Tbsp. of butter, let it melt and cook the last two pieces of chicken the same way.

7. Spread marinara sauce over the chicken breasts, top with the mozzarella cheese and sprinkle the remaining ½ tsp. Italian seasoning over the top. Place under the broiler for about 2 minutes or until the cheese is melted. Top with the basil and serve.

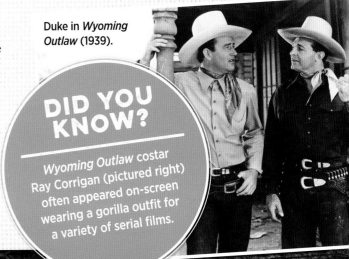

Duke in *Wyoming Outlaw* (1939).

DID YOU KNOW?

Wyoming Outlaw costar Ray Corrigan (pictured right) often appeared on-screen wearing a gorilla outfit for a variety of serial films.

OUTDOOR COOKING

These recipes make for smooth sailing when you're roughin' it.

Skillet Spaghetti and
Meatballs, pg. 150

MASTERING THE GREAT OUTDOORS

Follow these tips to make sure you get the most out of your cast-iron cookware on your next camping trip.

BE PREPARED

For many people, the appeal of camping out lies with spending a few days sleeping under the stars and away from the responsibilities of everyday life. But without proper preparation, your rustic adventure could be a hungry one. Before leaving, try planning what meals you want to cook and prepare as many of the ingredients ahead of time as possible. Chopping and portioning any vegetables, for instance, is going to be easier in your kitchen than at a campsite. Just make sure to pack whatever you've prepared in sealable plastic bags or other similar containers to keep it fresh for dinner time!

KEEP IT COOL

You don't want to take any chances when it comes to keeping your perishables fresh. That cut of beef may have been fresh as a daisy when you packed it before heading off to the woods, but unless you take the proper precautions, it can quickly turn into a breeding ground for bacteria. Always freeze whatever meat you plan on taking with you to minimize its time outside the safe temperature zone of 40 degrees Fahrenheit and below, and try and pack it with blocks of ice (or ice packs) in a cooler.

DON'T BUILD A BONFIRE

While a roaring fire may make for a beautiful sight, you're better off keeping things small when it comes to creating a suitable source of heat for your cast iron. If your campsite doesn't have a grill, you'll probably want to cook using heated coals rather than placing the cast iron directly over an open flame, as the former method allows for much better heat control. Build a fire as you normally would using small, dry twigs and branches as fuel, and then dig a nearby, separate, shallow hole surrounded by a ring of medium-sized stones to serve as your coal pit. As your fire burns and creates coals, move these hot little hunks with a metal tool brought specifically for this purpose into your handy coal pit. Arrange the coals in an even layer, put a small metal grate over the pit, and voilà!—you have a great source of heat on which to place your cast-iron and get cooking.

REMEMBER YOUR TIMING

Chances are, you're used to dealing with sources of heat far more predictable than what's available to you in the wild. Since even a bed of coals is likely hotter than what you work with in the kitchen, keep in mind there may be more of a "carryover cooking" factor in your meals than usual (that's when your food continues to cook after it is removed from its heat source). Bring along a meat thermometer to make sure your dinner is done just how you want it.

CLEAN UP

Make sure to practice good camping protocol of "leaving no trace" by making sure the fire is completely out, scattering any unused wood as naturally as possible. Also, gather the ashes and debris to scatter at a distance far away from the site.

COWBOY STEW

Take a page from the book of old trailhands and sit down to some stew on your next camping trip.

SERVES 8

PROVISIONS

- 1 lb. ground beef
- 1 lb. kielbasa sausage, cut into ¼-in. slices
- 1 medium white onion, diced
- 1 (10-oz.) can diced tomatoes and chilies, undrained
- 1 (15.5-oz.) can pinto beans, undrained
- 1 (15-oz.) can corn, drained
- 2 cups beef broth
- ½ cup steak sauce
- ½ cup mild taco sauce
- 2 Tbsp. chili powder
- 1 tsp. ground cumin

DIRECTIONS

1. Prepare the grill for direct and indirect heat. Put a cast-iron Dutch oven on the grill and preheat to medium (about 350 degrees F).

2. Place the ground beef in the bottom of the now preheated cast-iron Dutch oven and cook over direct heat, breaking up the beef, until no longer pink. Using paper towels, sop up any excess fat.

3. Add the sausage and onion and cook until the onions start to soften, about 5 minutes. Add the rest of the ingredients, keep over direct heat until hot, cover the Dutch oven, then move to the indirect heat side of the grill. Cover the grill, if possible, and let cook for 60 minutes, stirring occasionally.

A Martinez and John Wayne in *The Cowboys* (1972).

WAYNE FAMILY TIP

If you really want to up the spice level on this stew, you can switch out the mild taco sauce for one with a little more heat!

CAMPFIRE COCONUT RICE

Duke was never afraid of venturing off the beaten path when he felt it was worth it. Saddle up and expand your culinary horizons with this tasty dish.

SERVES 6

PROVISIONS

- 3 cups instant rice
- 1 (14-oz.) can full fat or light coconut milk
- 1 tsp. kosher or fine sea salt, plus more to taste
- 1½ Tbsp. butter
- 2 limes, zest finely grated and juiced
- ⅓ cup fresh cilantro leaves, minced

  Freshly ground black pepper, to taste

DIRECTIONS

1. Prepare the grill for direct heat and preheat to medium (350 degrees F).

2. Pour the rice into a 12-in. cast-iron skillet. Pour the coconut milk into a 4-cup measure and add enough water to make 3 cups total. Add 1 tsp. salt and pour the mixture over the rice. Stir to combine. Dot with the butter and cover the pan tightly with foil. Grill with the lid closed for 12 to 15 minutes. Remove from the grill, stir in the lime zest and juice and the minced cilantro, re-cover the pan with foil and let sit another 5 minutes. Remove the foil and fluff with a fork. Season to taste with salt and pepper.

DID YOU KNOW?

John Wayne played the character Stony Brooke, a member of the trio of adventurers called *The Three Mesquiteers*, in eight films (including *Three Texas Steers*).

John Wayne in *Three Texas Steers* (1939).

SKILLET SPAGHETTI AND MEATBALLS

Surprise your friends on the trail by serving them this Italian staple on your next trip.

SERVES 6

PROVISIONS

- 3 slices sandwich bread
- ½ cup milk
- 1 lb. ground beef
- 1 tsp. Italian seasoning
- 1½ tsp. kosher or fine sea salt
- ¾ tsp. pepper
- 2 Tbsp. olive oil
- 1 (24-oz.) jar marinara sauce
- 2½ cups water
- 12 oz. spaghetti
- 1 cup grated Parmesan cheese

DIRECTIONS

1. Prepare the grill for direct and indirect heat and preheat to medium-high (400 degrees F).

2. Crumble the bread into a large mixing bowl and cover with the milk. Let sit for 5 minutes. Add the ground beef, Italian seasoning, salt and pepper. Shape into small balls.

3. Place a 12-in. cast-iron skillet over direct heat and heat the oil. Brown the meatballs in batches until well browned on all sides. Remove from the skillet. Wipe the skillet out and place back over direct heat.

4. Add the marinara sauce and water to the skillet. Let heat until it starts to bubble gently, stirring.

5. Add the spaghetti and cook, stirring gently occasionally, until the spaghetti starts to soften. Add the meatballs back to the skillet, nestling them down into the sauce. Move the skillet over to the indirect heat side of the grill, cover the grill and cook until the pasta is just al dente, stirring gently occasionally. Once the spaghetti is almost done, sprinkle the cheese over the top, cover the grill and cook another 3 to 4 minutes.

John Wayne looks every inch a cowboy legend as he holds a pair of pistols.

WAYNE FAMILY TIP

To help you shape the perfect meatball, make sure your hands are wet when rolling—otherwise the meat will stick to your hands instead of forming a sphere.

RUSTIC JALAPEÑO POPPERS

These cheesy little morsels can help tide you over
until dinner is ready—or even serve as the main event on their own.

MAKES 24

PROVISIONS

- 12 large jalapeño peppers
- 4   oz. cream cheese, softened
- ½   cup grated cheddar cheese
- 8   slices thin cut bacon

DIRECTIONS

1. Prepare the grill for direct heat and preheat to medium.

2. Cut peppers in half lengthwise, scrape out the seeds and veins.

3. Combine the cream and cheddar cheeses in a mixing bowl. Divide the mixture evenly among the pepper halves.

4. Cut the bacon slices into thirds and wrap the peppers, making sure the seam is on the bottom of the pepper. Place in a cast-iron skillet. Place on the grill, cover the lid and cook for 15 to 20 minutes or until the bacon is browned and the cheese melted.

John Wayne in *Rio Grande* (1950).

DID YOU KNOW?

The movie *Rio Grande* is considered the final entry in director John Ford's Cavalry Trilogy, with the previous entries being 1948's *Fort Apache* and 1949's *She Wore a Yellow Ribbon*.

BACKWOODS CHICKEN

This finger-lickin' dish is sure to hit the spot after a long day on the trail.

SERVES 6

PROVISIONS

- 2 Tbsp. olive oil
- 1 medium white or yellow onion, diced
- 3 garlic cloves, minced
- 1 jalapeño pepper, deveined, seeded and minced
- 1 large sweet potato, peeled and diced
- 4 Tbsp. curry powder
- 1 (15-oz.) can diced fire-roasted tomatoes, undrained
- 4 cups chicken broth
- ¼ tsp. cayenne pepper, or to taste
  Kosher or fine sea salt, to taste
  Pepper, to taste
- 4 cups cooked chicken
- 3 cups baby spinach
  Rice for serving (optional)

DIRECTIONS

1. Prepare the grill for direct and indirect heat and preheat to medium-high (400-450 degrees F).

2. Pour oil into a cast-iron Dutch oven and heat until shimmering. Add the onion and cook, stirring occasionally, until soft and translucent, about 5 minutes. Add the garlic and jalapeño and cook for another minute. Add the sweet potato and curry powder and cook, stirring occasionally, for another 5 minutes. Add the tomatoes, chicken broth and cayenne. Bring to a boil, stirring occasionally. Cover the Dutch oven, move to the indirect heat side and simmer for 20 minutes or until the sweet potatoes are tender. Taste and season with salt and pepper. Add the chicken, cover the Dutch oven and cook until the chicken is heated through, about 5 minutes. Stir in the spinach and serve hot over rice, if desired.

John Wayne and Oliver Hardy smile with a furry costar in *The Fighting Kentuckian* (1949).

Duke in *The Sons of Katie Elder* (1965). The film was the first Duke made after undergoing a successful surgery to remove cancer from his lungs.

WAR WAGON CASSEROLE

Like the Duke and Kirk Douglas classic, this recipe is sure to be a favorite.

SERVES 8

PROVISIONS

FILLING

- 1 lb. ground chuck
- 1 tsp. salt
- ¾ tsp. pepper
- 1 tsp. garlic powder
- 1 tsp. onion powder
- 1 (15-oz.) can navy beans, undrained
- 1 (15-oz.) can dark red kidney beans, undrained
- 1 (15-oz.) can corn, undrained
- 1 cup barbecue sauce

CORNBREAD TOPPING

- 1⅓ cups cornmeal
- 1⅓ cups flour
- 1½ tsp. baking powder
- ½ tsp. baking soda
- ½ tsp. kosher or fine sea salt
- 1½ cups buttermilk
- ⅓ cup sugar
- 3 large eggs, lightly beaten

DIRECTIONS

1. Prepare the grill for direct and indirect heat and preheat to medium-high. Place a cast-iron Dutch oven on the grill, close the lid and let it come to temperature.

2. Put the ground chuck into the now preheated Dutch oven and sprinkle on salt, pepper, garlic powder and onion powder. Cook until no longer pink, breaking it up with a spoon or spatula. Move the cooked beef to one side of the pan and soak up the extra fat with paper towels.

3. Add both cans of beans, the corn and barbecue sauce. Stir to combine, close the lid and cook for 10 to 15 minutes or until bubbly.

4. In a medium mixing bowl, combine the cornmeal, flour, baking powder, baking soda and salt. Add the buttermilk, sugar and eggs and mix well. Spoon the batter on top of the beef and bean mixture and spread into an even layer. Close the lid of the grill and cook for 5 minutes. Using the back of a large metal spoon, redistribute the cornmeal batter over the top, as it tends to want to form in the middle. Cook 5 more minutes with the lid closed, spread the cornmeal mixture over the top again and move the Dutch oven to the indirect side of the grill. Cover the grill and cook for another 15 to 20 minutes or until the cornbread topping is set. Let sit off the heat for 5 minutes, garnish with green onions and serve.

Kirk Douglas and John Wayne in *The War Wagon* (1967).

159

CHICKEN ENCHILADA SKILLET

Your campfire meal just got a little hotter with this spicy classic.

SERVES 6

PROVISIONS

- 1 tsp. ground cumin
- 1 tsp. kosher or fine sea salt
- ½ tsp. pepper
- 2 large boneless skinless chicken breasts (about ¾ lb.)
- 1½ Tbsp. olive oil
- 1 (10-oz.) can diced tomatoes and chilies, undrained
- 1 (10-oz.) can red enchilada sauce
- 4 cups corn tortilla chips
- 2 cups grated Monterey Jack cheese
- 1 avocado, diced
- ½ cup fresh cilantro leaves

DIRECTIONS

1. Prepare the grill for direct heat. Place a cast-iron skillet on the grill and preheat the grill to medium-high (400 to 450 degrees F).

2. In a large mixing bowl, combine the cumin, salt and pepper. Cut the chicken breasts into bite-sized pieces and toss to coat well. Add the olive oil and stir.

3. Dump the chicken into the now preheated skillet, even out into a single layer and cook, stirring occasionally, until the chicken is cooked through, about 5 minutes.

4. Add the diced tomatoes and chilies to the skillet and cook for 1 minute, stirring. Add the enchilada sauce, stir and crush the tortilla chips into the skillet with your hands, breaking them into bite-sized pieces. Stir, cover the grill, and cook for 4 minutes. Stir, sprinkle the cheese all over the top, close the lid and cook for another 2 minutes or until the cheese has melted.

5. Let sit for 5 minutes off the heat. Sprinkle with avocado and cilantro, and serve.

John Wayne and others sing in a scene from *Westward Ho* (1935).

WAYNE FAMILY TIP

Not everyone loves the taste of cilantro. If you have some picky cowpokes with you on the trail, feel free to omit the flavorful herb in this recipe.

CAMPFIRE COBBLER

This dessert is a perfect way to end an evening spent under the stars.

SERVES 6

PROVISIONS

- 2 cups biscuit mix
- 1 cup sugar, divided
- 1½ cups milk
- 6 Tbsp. butter
- 2 cups peach slices, fresh or frozen and thawed
- 1 cup pitted sweet cherries, fresh or frozen and thawed

DIRECTIONS

1. Prepare the grill for direct and indirect heat, preheated to medium (350 degrees F).

2. In a mixing bowl, combine the biscuit mix with ¾ cup sugar. Add the milk and stir to combine.

3. Place the butter in a 9-in. cast-iron skillet. Place on the grill and heat until the butter melts. Add the biscuit batter to the pan and smooth into an even layer. The butter will bubble over the edges of the batter. Scatter the peaches and cherries over the top of the batter, sprinkle with the remaining ¼ cup sugar, close the lid and cook for 10 minutes. After 10 minutes, move the skillet to the indirect heat side, close the lid and cook for another 20 minutes or until a toothpick inserted into the center comes out clean.

Duke in *She Wore a Yellow Ribbon* (1949).

DID YOU KNOW?

Years after finishing the film *She Wore a Yellow Ribbon*, Duke maintained the script for that film was one of the best he had worked with in his career.

DUTCH OVEN CAKE

Think spending time in the great outdoors means missing out on cake? Think again, pardner.

SERVES 8

PROVISIONS

- 1 (21-oz.) can cherry pie filling
- 1 (20-oz.) can crushed pineapple in juice, undrained
- 1 box yellow cake mix
- 12 Tbsp. cold butter, cut into small pieces
- ¾ cup chopped pecans

DIRECTIONS

1. Prepare the grill for indirect heat and preheat to medium (350 degrees F).

2. Line a cast-iron Dutch oven with heavy duty aluminum foil. Place the cherry pie filling and pineapple, along with the juices, in the Dutch oven. Stir to combine. Sprinkle the cake mix evenly over the top. Dot the butter all over the top of the cake mix. Sprinkle with the pecans. Put the lid on the Dutch oven and cook on the grill, with the lid closed and maintaining a temperature of about 350 degrees F, for 55 to 65 minutes or until the cake topping is cooked through.

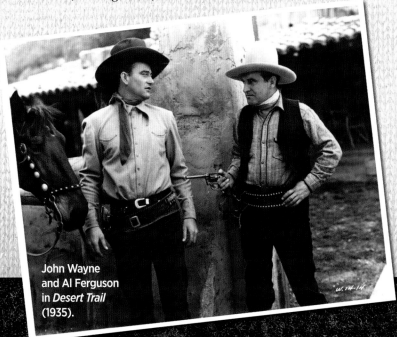

John Wayne and Al Ferguson in *Desert Trail* (1935).

FIRE BAKED APPLES

Make your next camping trip a little bit sweeter with these tasty apples.

SERVES 4

PROVISIONS

- 4 large crisp apples, such as Honey Crisps
- ½ cup brown sugar, packed
- 4 Tbsp. butter, softened
- ¼ cup dried cranberries, chopped
- ¼ cup walnuts, chopped
- 2 Tbsp. ground cinnamon
- 1 cup apple juice

DIRECTIONS

1. Prepare the grill for indirect heat, preheated to medium (350 degrees F).

2. Cut about a third off the top of each apple and use a spoon to scrape out the core and leave a well in the center.

3. In a small mixing bowl, combine the brown sugar, butter, cranberries, walnuts and cinnamon. Mix well. Stuff the mixture into the well of each apple.

4. Place the apples in a cast-iron Dutch oven. Pour the apple juice into the Dutch oven and add water if necessary to have the liquid come up to about ½-in. of the apples. Cover the Dutch oven and place on the grill. Cover the grill and let the apples cook for 40 to 50 minutes, or until the apples are tender but not falling apart. Check the apples halfway through to make sure there is still liquid in the pan, adding more if necessary.

John Wayne and George "Gabby" Hayes in *Dark Command* (1940).

DID YOU KNOW?

George "Gabby" Hayes had a long and successful career as a character actor in Western films, appearing in more than a dozen films with Duke, including *Dark Command*.

Perfect Pot
Roast, pg. 202

ALL IN ONE MEALS

Cut the kitchen clutter but keep the great taste.

ARROZ CON POLLO

The smell of this dish simmering in your cast iron means good eatin' is on its way.

SERVES 6 TO 8

PROVISIONS

- 4 tsp. kosher or fine sea salt
- 2 tsp. pepper
- 2 tsp. ground cumin
- 2 tsp. garlic powder
- 1 whole chicken, cut into 8 pieces
- 4 Tbsp. olive oil
- 1 large white or yellow onion, diced
- 1 green bell pepper, seeded, deveined and diced
- 3 garlic cloves, minced
- 2 Tbsp. double strength tomato paste
- 1 (16-oz.) bag yellow rice
- 4 cups water
- 1 (10-oz.) jar pimento stuffed olives, drained
- 1 roasted red bell pepper, cut into strips

DIRECTIONS

1. Put the salt, pepper, cumin and garlic powder in a large food storage bag. Add the chicken and shake well to coat the chicken with the spices.

2. Heat the oil in a large cast-iron Dutch oven over medium-high until it shimmers. Add the chicken, in batches, and brown well on both sides, about 5 to 6 minutes per side. Remove the chicken and place on a plate.

3. Add the onion and green pepper and cook, stirring, for 5 minutes or until tender. Add the garlic and cook, stirring, for 30 seconds. Add the tomato paste and cook, stirring, for 1 minute. Add the yellow rice and cook, stirring, for another minute. Add the chicken back to the Dutch oven and pour in water. Add the olives and stir. Bring to a boil, cover the pot, reduce the heat and simmer, stirring occasionally, for 45 minutes or until the rice has absorbed all the liquid. Place the red pepper strips on top and serve.

DID YOU KNOW?

John Wayne played Stony Brooke, a member of the "Three Mesquiteers," in eight films, including *Overland Stage Raiders*. After he moved on in 1939, actor Robert Livingston filled the role.

John Wayne, Ray Corrigan and Max Terhune in *Overland Stage Raiders* (1938).

BEEF STEW

A meal as delicious as it is simple, this stew will surely become a go-to.

SERVES 6

PROVISIONS

- 1½ lb. beef stew meat
- 2 Tbsp. Worcestershire sauce
- 1 tsp. garlic powder
- 1½ tsp. pepper, plus more to taste
- 3 tsp. kosher or fine sea salt, plus more to taste
- ½ cup flour
- 2 Tbsp. olive oil, plus more for cooking
- 1 large white onion, diced
- 1 lb. large carrots, peeled and cut into 2-in. pieces
- 1½ lb. small gold potatoes, scrubbed and cut in half
- 8 oz. whole white mushrooms, wiped clean, bottom of stem removed, and cut in half
- 1 Tbsp. double strength tomato paste
- 3½ cups beef broth
- 2 bay leaves
- 4 sprigs fresh thyme
- 1 tsp. minced fresh rosemary
- 1 (15-oz.) bag frozen baby peas

DIRECTIONS

1. Preheat oven to 275 degrees F.

2. Combine beef with Worcestershire sauce, garlic powder and ½ tsp. pepper in a mixing bowl and let sit for 15 minutes or until meat comes to room temperature.

3. Combine flour with 1 tsp. salt in a mixing bowl.

Add beef and toss well, making sure to coat each piece of beef with flour.

4. Pour enough olive oil into a cast-iron Dutch oven to coat the bottom. Heat over medium-high until it shimmers. Working in batches, brown the meat very well. Remove to a bowl or plate. Add more oil and let it heat up between batches. Once all the beef is browned, add 2 more Tbsp. oil to pan, let it heat up and add the onions, carrots, potatoes and mushrooms. Add 2 tsp. of salt, 1 tsp. of pepper and cook, stirring occasionally, for 10 minutes. Add tomato paste and cook, stirring, for 1 minute.

5. Return the beef to the Dutch oven, add the beef broth, bay leaves, thyme and rosemary, cover the Dutch oven, and bake for 2 hours or until the meat and vegetables are tender. Remove the bay leaves and thyme sprigs. Taste and add salt and pepper if needed. Stir in the peas and heat them through. Let sit a few minutes, then serve.

John Wayne in *The Big Stampede* (1932).

RED RIVER BRAISED SHORT RIBS

This tender and tasty meal could make even Tom Dunson smile.

SERVES 6

PROVISIONS

- 5 lb. boneless short ribs
- Kosher or fine sea salt, to taste
- Pepper, to taste
- 2 Tbsp. olive oil
- 3 large carrots, peeled and diced
- 1 large white or yellow onion, diced
- 2½ cups pineapple juice, divided
- 3–4 cups beef broth
- 1 chipotle pepper in adobo sauce, minced, plus 1 Tbsp. of the adobo sauce

DIRECTIONS

NOTE: BEGIN THIS RECIPE THE DAY BEFORE YOU PLAN TO SERVE.

1. Preheat oven to 325 degrees F.

2. Season the ribs generously on all sides with salt and pepper. Heat the oil in a cast-iron Dutch oven over high until the oil shimmers. Working in batches so as not to overcrowd the pan, brown the ribs well on all sides, about 5 minutes per side. Remove the ribs to a plate.

3. Add the carrots and onions to the pan and cook, stirring occasionally, until tender, about 5 minutes. Add 2 cups pineapple juice, 1 cup beef broth, the chipotle pepper and sauce to the pan. Bring to a boil, stirring occasionally. Add the ribs back to the pan along with any juices that have accumulated. Pour in enough beef broth so that the ribs are almost fully submerged. Cover the pan and bake for 3 hours or until the ribs are very tender. Remove from the heat and let cool.

4. Refrigerate the ribs in the pan overnight or up to 2 days.

ABOUT HALF AN HOUR BEFORE PLANNING TO SERVE

5. Remove the congealed fat from the top of the pan and discard. Place the Dutch oven on the stove over medium heat. Add ½ cup pineapple juice and heat the ribs. Taste and add more salt and pepper if needed.

DID YOU KNOW?

A celebrated actor of the stage, Montgomery Clift's second-ever Hollywood role was in *Red River*. The actor was able to hold his own opposite John Wayne, despite his inexperience.

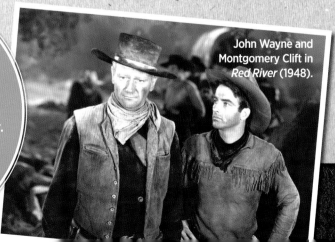

John Wayne and Montgomery Clift in *Red River* (1948).

CHISUM'S CHICKEN AND DUMPLINGS

Like a classic Duke movie, this meal will never leave you disappointed.

SERVES 6

PROVISIONS

- 2 Tbsp. olive oil
- 3 medium carrots, diced
- 1 large onion, diced
- 2 garlic cloves, minced
- 6 cups chicken broth
- 1 whole rotisserie chicken, skin and bones removed and shredded or chopped
- 2 bay leaves
- 2¼ tsp. kosher salt, divided
- ¾ tsp. pepper
- ¾ tsp. poultry seasoning
- 1½ cups flour
- 1 tsp. baking powder
- ½ tsp. baking soda
- 1½ tsp. sugar
- 2 Tbsp. butter, melted and cooled
- 1 cup (more or less) buttermilk
- Parsley or chives, chopped, for serving

DIRECTIONS

1. In a cast-iron Dutch oven, heat the olive oil over medium-high. Add the carrots and onion and cook until softened, about 5 minutes. Add the garlic and cook for another 30 seconds. Add the chicken broth, chicken and bay leaves, 1½ tsp. salt, pepper and poultry seasoning, stir and bring to a boil. Boil gently for 15 minutes.

2. In a mixing bowl, whisk together the flour, baking powder, baking soda, ¾ tsp. salt and the sugar. Add the melted butter and stir with a fork. Starting with about ¾ cup, stir in the buttermilk. Keep adding buttermilk, a little at a time, until the mixture forms into a soft dough.

3. Drop 1 Tbsp. of the batter at a time onto the top of the simmering soup, cover the pan and let simmer for 15 minutes or until the dumplings are cooked through.

4. Serve garnished with parsley or chives.

Duke and Lynda Day George in *Chisum* (1970).

WAYNE FAMILY TIP

One easy way to tell if your dumplings are cooked through is to poke them with a toothpick. If it comes out clean, your dumplings are done!

CHEESY CHICKEN AND CORN CHOWDER

If you like cheese, you're going to love chowing down on this chowder.

SERVES 8

PROVISIONS

- 4 slices thick cut bacon, chopped
- 1 large white or yellow onion, diced
- 2 lb. boneless skinless chicken breast, cut into 1-in. pieces
- 2 cups chicken broth
- 1 large Idaho potato, peeled and diced
- 2 cups milk
- 3 cups fresh or frozen (and thawed) corn kernels
- 3 sprigs fresh thyme
- 3–4 dashes hot sauce
- 8 oz. cheddar cheese, grated (about 2 cups grated)

  Kosher or fine sea salt, to taste

  Pepper, to taste

  Fresh parsley for garnish, if desired

DIRECTIONS

1. Place the bacon in a cold cast-iron Dutch oven, turn the heat to medium-low and cook gently, stirring occasionally, until the fat has rendered but the bacon is not crisp. Add the onions and cook until softened, stirring occasionally, about 5 minutes. Add the chicken, broth and potatoes, raise the heat and bring to a boil. Once the soup begins to boil, reduce the heat, cover and simmer for 12 to 14 minutes or until the chicken and potatoes are tender.

2. Add the milk, corn, thyme and hot sauce and heat gently until hot. Remove the thyme sprigs, stir in the cheese, and season to taste with salt and pepper. Cook, stirring, just until the cheese melts.

3. Garnish with sprigs of fresh parsley if desired.

DID YOU KNOW?

In *The Man Who Shot Liberty Valance* (1962), Duke stars alongside actor Lee Marvin. The two would appear on-screen together again the following year in *Donovan's Reef*.

From left: Lee Van Cleef, Lee Martin, Jimmy Stewart and John Wayne in *The Man Who Shot Liberty Valance*.

CHICKEN CHILE VERDE

This chicken dish is hot and spicy—just like John Wayne would have liked it!

SERVES 6 TO 8

PROVISIONS

- 1 Tbsp. olive oil
- 1 large white or yellow onion, diced
- 1 jalapeño pepper, seeded, deveined and minced
- 2 lb. ground chicken
- 1 tsp. kosher or fine sea salt
- 1 tsp. ground cumin
- ½ tsp. pepper
- 1 (4-oz.) can diced mild green chilies, drained
- 1 cup chicken broth
- 1 (16-oz.) jar salsa verde
- 1 cup sour cream

TO SERVE

Lime wedges

Fresh cilantro

Sliced jalapeño peppers

DIRECTIONS

1. Heat oil in a cast-iron Dutch oven over high. Add the onions and cook, stirring occasionally, until tender, about 2 to 3 minutes. Add the jalapeño pepper and cook for another minute, stirring. Add the chicken and cook, breaking it up with a spoon or spatula, until cooked through, 8 to 10 minutes. Add the salt, cumin, pepper and diced chilies, and cook, stirring for another minute. Add the chicken broth and salsa verde. Bring to a boil, lower the temperature and let simmer uncovered for 15 to 20 minutes. Remove from the heat and stir in the sour cream.

2. Serve with lime wedges, cilantro and sliced jalapeño peppers if desired.

John Wayne and Ella Raines in *Tall in the Saddle* (1944).

WAYNE FAMILY TIP

This recipe is so good, you'll want to enjoy every last mouthful. Serving this with a side of cornbread (such as Southern Cornbread on page 68) will help you soak up every last bit of deliciousness.

CHILI WITH BEANS

A favorite of cowboys for generations, chili is sure to please even the pickiest eater.

SERVES 6 TO 8

PROVISIONS

- 2 lb. ground chuck
- 2 Tbsp. chili powder
- 2 tsp. garlic powder
- 2 tsp. onion powder
- 1 tsp. kosher or fine sea salt
- 1 tsp. ground cumin
- ¼ tsp. cayenne powder
- 1 (10-oz.) can diced tomatoes and chili peppers, undrained
- 2 (8-oz.) cans tomato sauce
- 1½ cups beef broth, use divided
- ⅓ cup masa harina
- 1 (15.5-oz.) can pinto beans, rinsed and drained
- 1 (15.5-oz.) can kidney beans, rinsed and drained

FOR GARNISH

Grated cheddar

Tortilla chips

Sour cream

Chopped onions

Lime wedges

DIRECTIONS

1. Place the ground chuck in a cast-iron Dutch oven over high heat and brown well, about 5 minutes. Drain off any fat. Add the chili powder, garlic powder, onion powder, salt, cumin and cayenne powder and cook, stirring, until fragrant, about 1 minute. Add the diced tomatoes and chili peppers, tomato sauce and 1 cup beef broth. Reduce heat and simmer for 1 hour.

2. After 1 hour of simmering, whisk together the masa harina with ½ cup beef broth until it forms a smooth paste. Add to the chili along with the beans and cook for another 10 minutes, stirring occasionally.

3. Serve with grated cheese, chips, sour cream, chopped onions and lime wedges if desired.

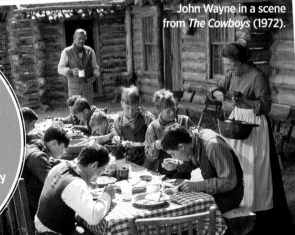

John Wayne in a scene from *The Cowboys* (1972).

DID YOU KNOW?

The Cowboys features one of the few times Duke dies on-screen! His character Wil Andersen is shot in the back by Bruce Dern's Asa Watts.

SKILLET CHILI WITH CORNBREAD TOPPING

Mixing together the cornbread and chili makes for perfect spoonfuls of tastiness.

SERVES 6

PROVISIONS

CHILI

- 1 Tbsp. olive oil
- 1 medium white or yellow onion, diced
- 2 garlic cloves, minced
- 1 lb. lean ground beef
- 4 Tbsp. tomato paste
- 1 (15-oz.) can diced tomatoes
- 1 Tbsp. chili powder
- 1 tsp. ground cumin
- 1 tsp. kosher or fine sea salt
- 1 tsp. dried oregano
- ½ tsp. pepper
- 1 (15-oz.) can kidney beans, rinsed and drained
- ½ cup beef broth

TOPPING

- 1 cup cornmeal
- 1 cup flour
- 1 tsp. baking powder
- ½ tsp. kosher or fine sea salt
- 2 tsp. sugar
- ½ cup melted butter
- 1 egg, lightly beaten
- 1 cup buttermilk

DIRECTIONS

1. Heat the oil in a cast-iron skillet over medium-high. Add the onions and cook until tender and translucent, about 5 minutes. Add the garlic and cook for another 30 seconds. Add the ground beef and cook, breaking up the beef with a spoon or spatula, and cook until no longer pink, about 5 minutes. Add the tomato paste and cook, stirring, for 1 minute. Add the rest of the ingredients, reduce heat and simmer for 15 minutes.

2. Preheat oven to 375 degrees F.

3. In a medium mixing bowl, combine the cornmeal, flour, baking powder, salt and sugar. Add the butter, egg and buttermilk and stir to combine. Smooth the topping over the top of the chili and bake for 30 minutes or until the crust is golden brown. Let cool slightly and serve.

John Wayne in *The Searchers* (1956).

WAYNE FAMILY TIP

If you find yourself out of kidney beans but still want to serve on this chili recipe, check and see if you have pinto beans—they make a fine replacement.

CORNED BEEF AND CABBAGE

One plateful of this recipe will knock your appetite across the pond.

SERVES 6 TO 8

PROVISIONS

1   (4-lb.) corned beef brisket (with seasoning packet)

2   bay leaves

1   tsp. black peppercorns

4   large yellow onions, peeled and quartered

1½ lb. carrots, peeled and quartered

8   medium red potatoes, scrubbed, eyes removed and halved

1   head of cabbage, trimmed and cut into 6 or 8 wedges

2   Tbsp. melted butter

2   Tbsp. minced fresh parsley

Kosher or fine sea salt, to taste

Freshly ground black pepper, to taste

DIRECTIONS

1. Place the corned beef and the seasoning it came with in a large cast-iron Dutch oven. Add the bay leaves and peppercorns. Cover with water, place the lid on the pot and bring to a boil. Once it starts to boil, reduce the heat and simmer for 2 hours. Add the onions, carrots and potatoes and continue to simmer for another 30 minutes or until the potatoes are tender. Remove the potatoes and place in a mixing bowl. Add the cabbage to the pot and continue to simmer for another 15 minutes or until the cabbage is tender.

2. Add the melted butter, parsley and a large pinch of salt and pepper to the potatoes. Toss to coat and keep warm while the cabbage cooks.

3. Remove the brisket and vegetables from the pot, slice the corned beef against the grain, and serve with the potatoes and vegetables.

DID YOU KNOW?

Victor McLaglen, who co-starred with Duke in *The Quiet Man*, had a son named Andrew who directed John Wayne in several films, including 1963's *McLintock!*

Duke and Victor McLaglen (along with others) in *The Quiet Man* (1952).

WHITE BEAN AND HAM SOUP

Sometimes, a cup of soup is just what you need to keep 'em satisfied.

SERVES 6 TO 8

PROVISIONS

- 1 lb. dried navy beans
- 2–3 smoked ham hocks
- 3 sprigs fresh thyme
- 2 bay leaves
- 2 large carrots, peeled and diced
- 1 large white onion, diced, plus more for serving
- 1 tsp. kosher or fine sea salt, plus more to taste
- 1 lb. fully cooked smoked ham steaks, medium diced

  Pepper, to taste

DIRECTIONS

1. Place the beans in a large bowl, add enough water to cover by 1 in. and let soak overnight. Drain and rinse the beans and place in a cast-iron Dutch oven along with the ham hocks, thyme and bay leaves. Add 3½ quarts of water. Bring to a boil and simmer, uncovered, for 1 hour.

2. After an hour of simmering, add the carrots, onions and 1 tsp. of salt. Cover the pot partially and continue to simmer, partially covered, for another hour. Stir occasionally. If too much water is evaporating, add more. Remove the thyme sprigs and bay leaves. Remove the ham hocks, place on a cutting board and, when cool enough to handle, remove the meat from the bones and add to the soup, discarding the skin and bones. Add the diced ham to the soup, season to taste with salt and pepper, and let simmer another 10 minutes before serving. Serve with diced fresh onion if desired.

John Wayne in *Flame of the Barbary Coast* (1945).

WAYNE FAMILY TIP

If you can't find smoked ham hocks, smoked turkey hocks make a decent substitute.

John Wayne, Montgomery Clift and Walter Brennan in *Red River* (1948). In 1940, Brennan won his third Best Supporting Actor Oscar for his performance in *The Westerner* (1940).

IRISH LAMB STEW

This simple but satisfying meal brings all the comforts of the Emerald Isle.

SERVES 6

PROVISIONS

- 1 Tbsp. kosher or fine sea salt, plus more to taste
- 1½ tsp. pepper, plus more to taste
- 1 tsp. garlic powder
- 3 lb. lamb shoulder, cut into 2-in. pieces
- 3 Tbsp. vegetable oil
- 6 small yellow onions, quartered
- 1 lb. baby carrots
- 1½ lb. baby gold potatoes, cut in half
- 4 sprigs fresh thyme
- 2 bay leaves
- 4 cups chicken broth
- 2 Tbsp. Worcestershire sauce

DIRECTIONS

1. Preheat oven to 350 degrees F.

2. In a large mixing bowl, combine 1 Tbsp. salt with 1½ tsp. pepper and the garlic powder. Stir to combine. Add the lamb and stir well, making sure to coat the lamb well with the seasoning.

3. Heat vegetable oil in a cast-iron Dutch oven over medium-high. Working in batches, add the lamb and brown well on all sides. Remove the lamb from the pot, add the onions and carrot and a large pinch of salt and pepper. Cook, stirring occasionally, until the vegetables start to brown, about 5 minutes. Add the lamb and any accumulated juices back to the pot. Top with the potatoes. Season the potatoes with a pinch of salt and pepper. Add the thyme, bay leaves, chicken broth and Worcestershire sauce. It is OK if everything is not submerged. Cover the pot and bake for 1½ hours or until the lamb and vegetables are tender.

John Wayne and Maureen O'Hara in *The Quiet Man* (1952).

DID YOU KNOW?

Republic Pictures only agreed to support director John Ford's passion project, *The Quiet Man*, because bankable star John Wayne promised to star in the film.

SKILLET LASAGNA

Everyone has their own take on this Italian staple. This is the best one yet.

SERVES 6

PROVISIONS

- 1 Tbsp. olive oil
- 1 medium white onion, diced
- 3 garlic cloves, minced
- 1 lb. Italian sausage, casings removed
- 1 (24-oz.) jar marinara sauce
- 2 (14.5-oz.) cans diced tomatoes, undrained
- 2 tsp. Italian seasoning, divided
- 8 oz. whole milk ricotta cheese
- 1½ cups grated Parmesan cheese, divided
- 5 oz. baby spinach, chopped
- 1 large egg
- 1 tsp. kosher or fine sea salt
- ½ tsp. pepper
- 6–8 no-boil lasagna noodles
- 8 oz. mozzarella cheese, grated

DIRECTIONS

1. Preheat oven to 400 degrees F.

2. Heat the oil in a 12-in. cast-iron skillet. Add the onion and cook, stirring occasionally, until softened, about 5 minutes. Add the garlic and cook, stirring, for 30 seconds. Add the sausage and cook, breaking it up with a spatula, until no longer pink, about 5 minutes. Add the marinara sauce, diced tomatoes and juice and 1 tsp. Italian seasoning. Lower the heat and let simmer for 10 minutes.

3. In a medium mixing bowl, combine the ricotta cheese with ½ cup Parmesan, the spinach, egg, remaining 1 tsp. Italian seasoning, salt and pepper. Mix well.

4. When the sauce has finished simmering, remove all but about ¾ cup and place in a bowl. Cover the sauce in the skillet with half the noodles, breaking them up to fit if needed. Spread half the ricotta cheese mixture evenly over the noodles, then top with half the remaining sauce and half the grated mozzarella. Repeat the layers one more time. Sprinkle the remaining Parmesan cheese over the top and bake for 30 to 40 minutes or until the sauce is bubbly and the cheese has melted and started to brown. Let cool 10 minutes before serving.

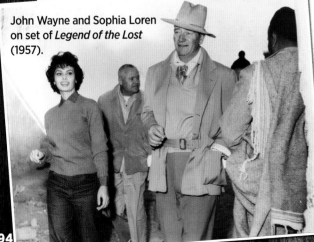

John Wayne and Sophia Loren on set of *Legend of the Lost* (1957).

ONE POT SPAGHETTI

Whip together this pasta and bring a little of the old country to your table.

SERVES 4

PROVISIONS

- 1 Tbsp. olive oil
- 2 tsp. anchovy paste
- 1 shallot, thinly sliced
- 1 garlic clove, minced
- 12 oz. spaghetti
- 1 pint cherry tomatoes, cut in half
- ½ cup pitted Kalamata olives, cut in half
- 8 basil leaves, thinly sliced, divided
- ½ tsp. kosher or fine sea salt
- ½ tsp. red pepper flakes
- ½ tsp. pepper
- 4½ cups water
- 1 oz. Parmesan cheese

DIRECTIONS

1. Heat the olive oil in a 12-in. cast-iron skillet over medium. Add the anchovy paste and cook, stirring, until dissolved. Add the shallot and garlic and cook, stirring, for 1 minute. Place the spaghetti in the skillet, add the tomatoes, olives, half the basil, salt, red pepper flakes, pepper and water. Turn heat to high, bring to a boil and boil, stirring with tongs or forks, until the water has mostly evaporated and the pasta is cooked, about 10 minutes. Grate half the cheese over the pasta, stir and then grate the rest of cheese over and sprinkle on the remaining basil leaves.

2. Serve immediately.

John Wayne and Dean Martin cook while filming *The Sons of Katie Elder* (1965).

DID YOU KNOW?

John Wayne and Dean Martin starred together in two films—*Rio Bravo* (1959) and *The Sons of Katie Elder* (1965).

CHICKEN AND CHORIZO PAELLA

This hearty dish comes with a little zip of heat, courtesy of Duke.

SERVES 4 TO 6

PROVISIONS

PAELLA

- 3 Tbsp. olive oil
- 1 large white onion, diced
- 1 large carrot, peeled and diced
- 3 garlic cloves, minced
- ½ lb. fresh chorizo
- 4 boneless, skinless chicken thighs, cut into bite-sized pieces
- 1 red bell pepper, seeded, deveined and diced
- 1½ cups whole grain brown rice
- 3 cups chicken broth
- 1 cup frozen baby peas (no need to defrost)
- ½ cup chopped parsley
  Lemon wedges

SPICY AIOLI

- ½ cup mayonnaise
- 1½ tsp. sriracha sauce
  Juice of ½ lemon
- 1 small or ½ large garlic clove, grated or very finely minced

DIRECTIONS

PAELLA

1. Heat the oil in a 12-in. cast-iron skillet over medium-high. Add the onions and carrots, and cook, stirring occasionally, until the onions soften and start to brown. Add the garlic and cook, stirring, for 30 seconds. Remove the chorizo from the casing and crumble into the pan. Add the chicken and pepper and cook, stirring, for 5 minutes. Add the rice and chicken broth, stir and bring to a boil. Reduce heat to medium and cook, uncovered, until the rice has absorbed all the liquid, about 16 minutes. Adjust heat as necessary to keep from boiling. Stir in the peas and let sit for 5 minutes before serving.

2. Serve garnished with parsley and lemon wedges, with the aioli on the side.

SPICY AIOLI

1. Mix all ingredients together in a small bowl. Transfer to a small serving bowl, cover with plastic wrap and refrigerate until serving time. Eat the paella with a dollop of aioli on top and a squeeze of lemon juice.

John Wayne in a scene from *The Comancheros* (1961).

WAYNE FAMILY TIP

Don't be afraid to shift the pan around when cooking the paella if you feel the whole pan isn't being heated evenly. There's nothing worse than a half-cooked meal!

PORK CHOPS WITH BLACK BEANS AND RICE

Pig out with this delicious combo of beans, rice and chops.

SERVES 4

PROVISIONS

- 2 tsp. kosher or fine sea salt
- 1 tsp. pepper
- 1 tsp. ground cumin
- 8 bone-in pork chops
- 2 Tbsp. olive oil
- 1 large white onion, diced
- 2 garlic cloves, minced
- 1 cup uncooked whole grain brown rice
- 1 cup chicken broth
- 1 cup orange juice
- 1 (15-oz.) can black beans, drained and rinsed
- 3 Tbsp. roughly chopped fresh cilantro, to garnish
- Orange wedges, to garnish

DIRECTIONS

1. In a small bowl, combine the salt, pepper and cumin. Sprinkle the mixture on both sides of the pork chops.

2. Heat the oil in a 12-in. cast-iron skillet over medium high and brown the pork chops well on both sides, about 5 minutes per side. Remove the pork chops from the pan and place on a plate.

3. Add the onion and cook, stirring occasionally, until tender and just beginning to brown, about 5 minutes. Add the garlic and cook, stirring, for 30 seconds. Add the rice and cook, stirring, for 1 minute. Add the chicken broth, orange juice and black beans, then stir to combine. Place the pork chops back into the skillet, lower the heat to medium-low and cook for 10 minutes. Flip the pork chops over and continue to cook until the rice has absorbed all the liquid and the pork is cooked through, about 10 more minutes.

4. Garnish with cilantro and orange wedges.

Ben Johnson, Ann-Margret and John Wayne in *The Train Robbers* (1973).

DID YOU KNOW?

The Train Robbers was one of the last films produced by John Wayne's own production company, Batjac Productions.

PERFECT POT ROAST

This tasty classic will have you counting the hours until dinnertime.

SERVES 6

PROVISIONS

1 (3-lb.) boneless chuck roast

   Kosher or fine sea salt, to taste

   Pepper, to taste

2 Tbsp. olive oil

4 garlic cloves, minced

4 sprigs fresh thyme

2 sprigs fresh rosemary

3 cups beef broth, divided

2 bay leaves

6 large carrots, peeled and cut into 2-in. pieces

2 lb. baby Yukon gold or red potatoes, left whole

1 (16-oz.) bag frozen whole pearl onions

2 Tbsp. flour

John Wayne in *Rio Grande* (1950).

DIRECTIONS

1. Remove the roast from the refrigerator about 20 minutes before beginning to cook and season generously on all sides with salt and pepper.

2. Preheat oven to 300 degrees F. Heat the oil in a cast-iron or enameled cast-iron Dutch oven over medium-high until it begins to shimmer. Add the chuck roast and brown well on all sides, about 5 minutes per side. Remove the chuck from the pan, then add the garlic, thyme and rosemary and cook for 30 seconds. Add 1 cup beef broth and deglaze the pan, scraping the bottom of the pan with a whisk.

3. Return the beef to the pan, add the remaining beef broth and bay leaves, cover and bake for 1½ hours. Add the carrots, potatoes and onions to the pot, cover and bake for another 1½ hours or until the beef and vegetables are tender. With a slotted spoon, remove the vegetables to a serving platter. Remove the beef, add to the platter and cover with foil to keep warm. Place the Dutch oven on the stove top over high heat. Remove about ¼ cup of the liquid, whisk in the flour, add back to the pot and bring to a boil. Boil gently, whisking, until the gravy thickens. Slice the meat and serve the gravy alongside the meat and vegetables.

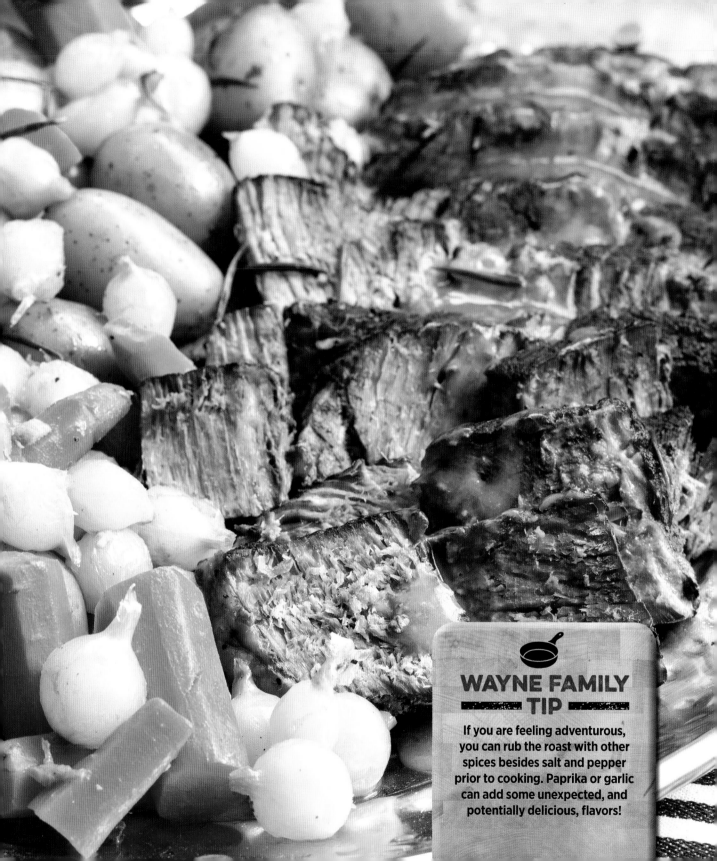

WAYNE FAMILY TIP

If you are feeling adventurous, you can rub the roast with other spices besides salt and pepper prior to cooking. Paprika or garlic can add some unexpected, and potentially delicious, flavors!

RED HOT TEXAS CHILI

This stew may be hotter than a summer afternoon in the desert, but the flavor is worth it!

SERVES 6 TO 8

PROVISIONS

- 2 oz. dried New Mexico or California red chilies
- 3 garlic cloves, chopped
- 1½ tsp. dried cumin
- 1 tsp. kosher or fine sea salt, plus more to taste
- 1 tsp. pepper, plus more to taste
- 1 Tbsp. brown sugar, packed
- 1 chipotle in adobo sauce with 1 Tbsp. sauce (omit if you don't want your chili really spicy)
- 2¼ cups beef broth, use divided
- 2½ lb. chuck, cut into bite-sized pieces
- 5 Tbsp. vegetable oil
- 1 large white or yellow onion, diced
- 2 Tbsp. masa harina
- 2 cups water
  Grated cheddar cheese (optional)
  Sour cream (optional)

DIRECTIONS

1. Remove the stems and seeds from the dried peppers and, in a heatproof bowl, cover with boiling water. Let sit for 15 minutes or until soft and pliable. Drain.

2. Place the rehydrated peppers in a blender or small food processor with the garlic, cumin, 1 tsp. salt, 1 tsp. pepper, brown sugar and chipotle if using. Add ¼ cup beef stock and process until smooth.

3. Season the chuck with salt and pepper. Heat 2 Tbsp. of oil in a cast-iron Dutch oven over medium-high until it begins to shimmer. Add half the beef and brown well on all sides. Remove the beef with a slotted spoon and place on a plate. Add another 2 Tbsp. of oil and heat. Brown the rest of the beef and remove to the plate.

4. Add the remaining Tbsp. of oil and cook the onions, stirring occasionally, until tender, about 5 minutes. Add the chili paste you made and cook, stirring, for another minute. Add the beef and any accumulated juices back into the pan. Add the beef broth. Whisk the masa harina into about ½ cup water and add to the pan with the rest of the water. Bring to a simmer over high heat then lower the heat and simmer gently for 2 hours uncovered or until the liquid has thickened slightly and the beef is tender. If the chili looks too dry, add more water or broth as needed.

5. Serve with grated cheese and sour cream if desired.

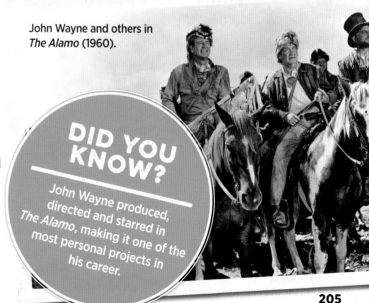

John Wayne and others in *The Alamo* (1960).

DID YOU KNOW?

John Wayne produced, directed and starred in *The Alamo*, making it one of the most personal projects in his career.

SAUSAGE SKILLET DINNER

Sure, this dish makes for a great evening meal, but it tastes good enough to eat anytime of the day!

SERVES 6

PROVISIONS

- 2   Tbsp. olive oil
- 1   large white onion, diced
- 1   red bell pepper, seeded, deveined and diced
- 2   garlic cloves, minced
- 1   kielbasa sausage, cut into ¼-in. slices
- 2   cups broccoli florets
- ¾   cup instant rice
- 1½ cups chicken broth
- 8   oz. grated sharp cheddar cheese (2 cups grated)
-     Kosher or fine sea salt, to taste
-     Pepper, to taste

DIRECTIONS

1. Heat oil in a cast-iron skillet over medium-high. Add the onion and red pepper and cook, stirring occasionally, until tender, about 5 minutes. Add the garlic and cook, stirring, for 30 seconds. Add the sausage and cook until starting to brown. Stir in the broccoli.

2. Add the rice and chicken broth, stir to combine, lower the heat to medium-low and cook until the rice has absorbed the liquid. Remove from the heat and stir in the cheese until melted. Season to taste with salt and pepper.

John Wayne in *Three Texas Steers* (1939).

WAYNE FAMILY TIP

While we love cheddar, feel free to experiment with different cheeses in this dish, such as pepper jack!

TEX MEX SKILLET MAC AND CHEESE

This creamy dish comes with a kick of spice, making it a favorite on both sides of the border.

SERVES 6

PROVISIONS

- 1 lb. short cut pasta such as elbows, spirals or bow ties
- 1 tsp. kosher or fine sea salt, plus more to taste
- 3 cups water
- 1 (12-oz.) can evaporated milk
- 1 (10-oz.) can diced tomatoes and green chilies, undrained
- 1 cup grated Monterey Jack cheese
- 1 cup grated cheddar cheese
- Pepper, to taste
- Paprika, to garnish

DIRECTIONS

1. Combine the pasta, 1 tsp. of salt and water in a large cast-iron skillet. Bring to a boil over high heat. Cook, stirring occasionally, until almost all of the water is gone and the pasta is tender.

2. Add the evaporated milk and tomatoes. Bring to a boil. Reduce heat to medium and cook until the mixture thickens, about 5 minutes. Add the cheeses and cook, stirring, until the cheese is melted. Add additional salt and pepper to taste. Sprinkle the top with paprika and serve.

John Wayne in *The Alamo* (1960).

DID YOU KNOW?

John Wayne constructed a huge set for *The Alamo* in Brackettville, Texas, that was so lifelike that it served as a tourist attraction for decades!

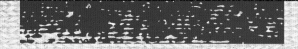

VINEGAR BRAISED CHICKEN

Don't settle for anything less than the best—pick this dish for dinner tonight!

SERVES 4 TO 6

PROVISIONS

- 1 Tbsp. kosher or fine sea salt
- 2 tsp. garlic powder
- 1 tsp. pepper
- 8 bone-in, skin-on chicken thighs
- 4 slices thick cut bacon, cut into small pieces
- 1 (14-oz.) bag frozen whole pearl onions, thawed
- ¾ cup sherry or red wine vinegar
- ¾ cup balsamic vinegar
- 2 cups chicken broth
- 4 sprigs fresh thyme, plus more for garnish
- 2 bay leaves
- 1 Tbsp. honey

DIRECTIONS

1. In a small bowl, combine the salt, garlic powder and pepper. Rinse the chicken and dry well with paper towels. Season with the spice mixture on both sides and let sit while the bacon cooks.

2. Place the bacon in a cold 12-in. cast-iron skillet. Turn the heat to medium and cook, stirring occasionally, until the bacon has rendered the fat and is crispy. Remove from the pan with a slotted spoon and place on paper towels to drain. Reserve for serving.

3. Increase the heat to medium-high, add the chicken to the hot bacon fat and, working in batches so as to not overcrowd the pan, brown well on both sides. Remove the chicken to a plate or bowl. Once the chicken is browned, add the onions to the bacon fat and cook, stirring occasionally, until they start to brown, about 5 minutes. Push the onions to one side of the pan and use paper towels to sop up the grease, but leave as much of the brown bits at the bottom of the pan as possible. Add the vinegars to the pan, raise heat to high and bring to a boil. Let boil for 1 minute, stirring. Add the chicken broth, chicken, thyme and bay leaves, and bring to a boil. Reduce the heat and let simmer gently for 40 minutes.

4. With a slotted spoon, remove the chicken and onions from the skillet and place in a serving dish. Remove the bay leaves and thyme sprigs and pour the pan liquid into a 2-cup glass measuring cup. Let the fat rise to the top, skim it off, and pour the liquid back into the skillet. Add the honey, bring to a boil and let boil for 2 to 3 minutes or until the liquid starts to thicken slightly. Spoon the sauce over the chicken and onions, garnish with fresh thyme leaves and the bacon, and serve.

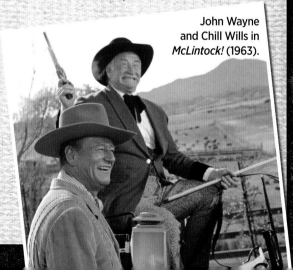

John Wayne and Chill Wills in *McLintock!* (1963).

Chocolate Bread
Pudding, pg. 220

DARN GOOD DESSERTS

These tasty treats hit the sweet spot every time.

BUCKIN' BERRY COBBLER

Hang tight! This cobbler packs a powerful kick of flavor.

SERVES 6 TO 8

PROVISIONS

FILLING

- ½ cup sugar
- 2 Tbsp. cornstarch
- 8 cups mixed berries (if using strawberries, limit to 1½ cups and cut them in half)
- Juice and finely grated zest of 1 lemon

DOUGH

- 1½ cups flour
- 4 Tbsp. sugar, divided
- 1½ tsp. baking powder
- ½ tsp. baking soda
- ½ tsp. kosher or fine sea salt
- 6 Tbsp. cold butter, cut into small pieces
- ¾ cup buttermilk

DIRECTIONS

1. Preheat oven to 375 degrees F.

2. Prepare the filling. Combine the sugar and cornstarch in a mixing bowl. Add the berries, lemon juice and zest, stir and let sit while preparing the dough.

3. For the dough, whisk together the flour, 3 Tbsp. sugar, baking powder, baking soda and salt. Add the butter and, using a pastry cutter or your fingers, work the butter into the flour until it resembles a coarse meal with some bigger pieces of butter. Add the buttermilk and stir until combined.

4. Pour the filling into a cast-iron skillet. Drop tablespoonfuls of the dough on top of the berries. Sprinkle the dough with 1 Tbsp. sugar. Bake for 40 to 50 minutes or until the dough is golden brown and the berries are bubbling. Let cool a little before serving.

John Wayne in *Ride Him, Cowboy* (1932).

WAYNE FAMILY TIP

Zest the lemon before juicing it. This ensures the strong flavor of the zest that would otherwise be lost if you squeezed first.

SKILLET BLUEBERRY POT PIE

Dig into this "berry" good dessert to end the day on a sweet note.

SERVES 6

PROVISIONS

- 1 Tbsp. butter, softened
- 48 oz. frozen blueberries (no need to thaw)
- 1½ cups plus 1 Tbsp. sugar, divided
- Juice of 1 lemon
- 5 Tbsp. cornstarch
- 7 Tbsp. water, divided
- 1 Tbsp. pure vanilla extract
- 1 premade piecrust
- 1 large egg

DIRECTIONS

1. Preheat oven to 350 degrees F. Grease a 12-in. cast-iron skillet generously with the butter.

2. In a large saucepan, combine the blueberries, 1½ cups sugar and lemon juice. Bring to a boil over high heat. Mix the cornstarch with 6 Tbsp. water and stir into the boiling blueberries. Let boil for 1 minute, stirring constantly, then take off the heat, stir in the vanilla and let cool slightly. Pour the blueberries into the prepared skillet.

3. Roll the dough out and cut a circle slightly larger than the skillet. Place the dough on top of the blueberries. Beat the egg with 1 Tbsp. water and, using a pastry brush, lightly wash the egg on top of the dough. Cut a small hole in the center of the dough to allow the steam to escape. Sprinkle the dough with the remaining tablespoon of sugar and bake for 40 to 50 minutes or until the crust is golden brown and the blueberries are bubbly. Serve warm.

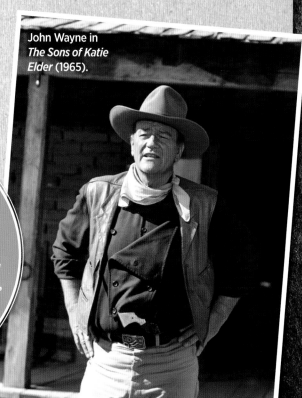

John Wayne in *The Sons of Katie Elder* (1965).

DID YOU KNOW?

The Sons of Katie Elder was the first film Duke made after undergoing a successful surgery to remove cancer from his lungs, and proved the life-saving operation didn't slow him down!

CHERRY SURPRISE

Nothing satisfies better than a big bite of this dessert.

SERVES 6

PROVISIONS

- 1   Tbsp. butter, softened
- ¾   cup plus 2 Tbsp. sugar, divided
- 3   cups pitted dark sweet cherries, fresh or frozen and thawed
- 2   cups milk
- 3   large eggs
- ¼   cup cornstarch
- 1   tsp. pure vanilla extract
- ½   tsp. pure almond extract
- ¼   tsp. kosher or fine sea salt
-     Powdered sugar, to serve

DIRECTIONS

1. Preheat oven to 375 degrees F.

2. Grease a 9-in. cast-iron skillet generously with the butter. Sprinkle 2 Tbsp. of sugar over the butter, then add the cherries to the skillet.

3. In a blender, combine the remaining ¾ cup sugar, milk, eggs, cornstarch, extracts and salt. Blend until smooth. Pour over the cherries and bake for 40 minutes or until puffed and golden. Dust with powdered sugar and serve immediately.

John Wayne in a scene from *Stagecoach* (1939).

CHOCOLATE BREAD PUDDING

Chocolate and bread come together in one delicious dessert.

SERVES 8 TO 10

PROVISIONS

- 1 Tbsp. butter, softened
- 6 large eggs
- 3 cups chocolate milk
- ½ cup brewed coffee, cooled
- ½ cup light brown sugar, lightly packed
- ¼ cup heavy cream
- 1 Tbsp. pure vanilla extract
- 4 Tbsp. unsweetened cocoa powder
- 1 loaf white sandwich bread, cut into 1-in. cubes
- 1 cup semi-sweet or bittersweet chocolate chips

DIRECTIONS

1. Preheat oven to 325 degrees F. Grease a 12-in. cast-iron skillet with the butter.

2. Whisk the eggs in a large mixing bowl. Add the chocolate milk, coffee, brown sugar, cream and vanilla, and whisk well. Whisk in the cocoa powder. Add the bread, stir and let sit for 15 to 20 minutes, stirring occasionally. Pour the bread mixture into the prepared skillet, add the chocolate chips and stir to distribute the chips throughout. Bake for 1 hour or until the custard is set and the top browned.

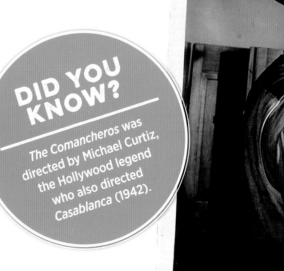

DID YOU KNOW?

The Comancheros was directed by Michael Curtiz, the Hollywood legend who also directed Casablanca (1942).

Duke in *The Comancheros* (1961).

SKILLET CHOCOLATE CHIP COOKIES

If you like chocolate chip cookies (and who doesn't?),
then we've found the right dessert for you.

SERVES 6

PROVISIONS

1½ cups flour

1½ tsp. baking powder

½ tsp. salt

12 Tbsp. butter, at room temperature

1   cup light brown sugar, lightly packed

½ cup sugar

2   large eggs, at room temperature

2   tsp. pure vanilla extract

1½ cups semi-sweet or bittersweet chocolate chips

DIRECTIONS

1. Preheat oven to 325 degrees F.

2. Whisk together the flour, baking powder and salt in a medium mixing bowl.

3. Place the butter and sugars into the bowl of an electric mixer preferably fitted with a paddle attachment. Beat on medium-high speed until light and fluffy, about 3 minutes. Add the eggs, one at a time, beating well after each addition. Beat in the vanilla. Turn the mixture to low and add the flour mixture. Beat just until the dough starts to come together, Add the chocolate chips and stir in well with a spatula, making sure you scrape the sides and bottoms of the bowl.

4. Divide the mixture into three 5-in. cast-iron skillets or one 9-in. skillet. Bake small skillets for 20 to 25 minutes, 35 to 30 minutes in a large skillet, or until golden and set.

John Wayne in
True Grit (1969).

SKILLET HOT FUDGE PUDDING CAKE

Three ways to guarantee a great recipe?
Chocolate, chocolate and more chocolate.

SERVES 6

PROVISIONS

- 6 Tbsp. butter
- ½ cup bittersweet chocolate chips
- 7 Tbsp. unsweetened cocoa powder, divided
- 1¼ cups sugar, use divided
- ¾ cup flour
- 2 tsp. baking powder
- ½ tsp. kosher or fine sea salt
- ½ cup milk
- 1 large egg
- 2 tsp. pure vanilla extract
- ½ cup brown sugar, packed
- 1½ cups hot brewed coffee
- 1 cup heavy cream, whipped to soft peaks

DIRECTIONS

1. Preheat oven to 325 degrees F.

2. Place the butter, chocolate chips and 3 Tbsp. cocoa powder in a skillet over low heat. Cook, stirring, until the butter is fully melted and the mixture is smooth. Let cool slightly.

3. In a medium mixing bowl, whisk together ¾ cup sugar, the flour, baking powder and salt. Add the milk, egg and vanilla and whisk. Add to the skillet with the chocolate and whisk until fully combined.

4. In a small mixing bowl, combine the remaining ½ cup sugar, remaining 4 Tbsp. cocoa powder and the brown sugar. Sprinkle over the cake batter in an even layer. Pour the hot coffee on and do not stir. Bake for 35 minutes or until the edges of the cake come away from the pan. Place the skillet on a wire rack and cool for 15 minutes before serving. Spoon some of the sauce from the bottom of the skillet over each piece of cake and dollop with whipped cream.

Duke in *3 Godfathers* (1948).

DID YOU KNOW?

Although John Ford made *3 Godfathers* in 1948, that wasn't the first time Hollywood adapted Peter Kyne's novel. A 1936 version starred beloved character actor Walter Brennan.

CHURROS WITH CHOCOLATE DIPPING SAUCE

How do you make one of Mexico's best-tasting treats taste even better? By adding chocolate.

SERVES 6 TO 8

PROVISIONS

CHOCOLATE DIPPING SAUCE

- ¾ cup good quality semi-sweet chocolate chips
- ⅔ cup heavy cream
- 1 Tbsp. light corn or agave syrup
- 1 tsp. pure vanilla extract

CHURROS

- 1½ cups plus ¼ cup sugar, divided
- 3 Tbsp. ground cinnamon
- 4 cups vegetable oil
- 4 large eggs
- 1 cup water
- 1 stick butter (½ cup)
- ⅛ tsp. kosher or fine sea salt
- 1 cup flour

DIRECTIONS

CHOCOLATE DIPPING SAUCE

1. Combine the chocolate chips, cream and corn syrup in a heavy bottomed, small saucepan and heat over low heat, stirring occasionally, until the chocolate is fully melted. Take off the heat and stir in the vanilla. Let cool while making the churros.

CHURROS

1. Combine 1½ cups sugar and the cinnamon in a large mixing bowl.

2. Pour the oil into a cast-iron Dutch oven and heat to 350 degrees F over medium heat.

3. Assemble ingredients before starting. Break the eggs into a liquid measuring cup or spouted pitcher. Place the water, butter, ¼ cup sugar and salt in a heavy saucepan over medium-high heat. Bring to a simmer. Add the flour all at once and stir with a wooden spoon until it forms a thick dough. Continue to cook while stirring for about 1 minute.

4. Dump the dough into the bowl of an electric mixer preferably fitted with a paddle attachment. Mix on low speed for a minute to cool the dough slightly. Add the eggs, one at a time, mixing well after each addition. After all the eggs have been added continue to mix, increasing the speed to medium-high, until the dough is smooth, thick and shiny, about 2 or 3 minutes.

5. Put the dough into a pastry bag with a large round or star tip and pipe out 6-in. lengths of dough directly into the hot oil. Fry for 2 to 3 minutes per side or until golden brown. Remove with a slotted spoon, let the excess oil drip off, then place the churros into the cinnamon sugar mixture. Toss gently to coat. Continue until all the dough is cooked. Serve with the chocolate dipping sauce.

John Wayne in *Rio Lobo* (1970).

Harry Carey Jr.,
Duke and Pedro
Armendáriz in
3 Godfathers (1948).

PILGRIM'S PEACH COBBLER

This dessert is sweet enough to keep you coming back for seconds....and thirds, fourths and fifths!

SERVES 6

PROVISIONS

- 1 cup flour
- 1 cup sugar
- 1 tsp. baking powder
- ½ tsp. kosher or fine sea salt
- 1 cup milk
- ½ cup butter
- 3 cups sliced peaches, fresh or frozen and thawed

  Fresh or whipped cream for serving, if desired

DIRECTIONS

1. Preheat oven to 350 degrees F.

2. In a medium mixing bowl, whisk together the flour, sugar, baking powder and salt. Whisk in the milk.

3. Melt the butter in cast-iron skillet. Pour in the batter and scatter the peaches on top. Bake for 30 to 40 minutes or until the batter is set and golden brown.

John Wayne in *The Man Who Shot Liberty Valance* (1962).

DID YOU KNOW?

In 1962, singer Gene Pitney released the song "The Man Who Shot Liberty Valance" (written by Burt Bacharach), although the tune was not featured in the film.

PINEAPPLE UPSIDE DOWN CAKE

Say "aloha"—which means "hello" and "goodbye" in Hawaiian, to this dessert.
It won't be sticking around for long!

SERVES 6 TO 8

PROVISIONS

- 12 Tbsp. butter, divided
- 1 cup brown sugar, lightly packed
- 1 (20-oz.) can pineapple rings in juice, drained and ¼ cup juice reserved
- 1 jar maraschino cherries
- 1¼ cups flour
- ½ cup yellow cornmeal
- 2 tsp. baking powder
- ½ tsp. kosher or fine sea salt
- ½ tsp. baking soda
- ¾ cup sugar
- ½ cup buttermilk
- 2 large eggs
- 2 tsp. pure vanilla extract

DIRECTIONS

1. Preheat oven to 350 degrees F.

2. Melt 4 Tbsp. of butter over low heat in a cast-iron skillet. Remove from heat and sprinkle the brown sugar over the butter in an even layer. Place the drained pineapple slices over the brown sugar and place a maraschino cherry in the center of each pineapple ring.

3. In a large mixing bowl, combine the flour, cornmeal, baking powder, salt and baking soda. In another mixing bowl, whisk together ¼ cup of the reserved pineapple juice, the sugar, buttermilk, eggs and vanilla. Melt the remaining 8 Tbsp. of butter and whisk into the batter. Mix the flour mixture into the wet ingredients. Pour the batter over the pineapple rings. Bake for 30 to 40 minutes or until a toothpick inserted in the center comes out clean. Run a dinner knife around the edges of the skillet, place a cake platter on top of the skillet and flip over.

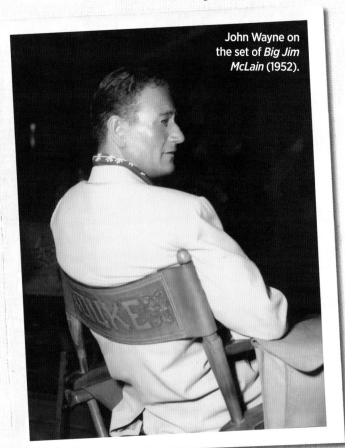

John Wayne on the set of *Big Jim McLain* (1952).

WAYNE FAMILY TIP

If peaches are your fruit of choice, they can be easily substituted for pineapple. Instead of canned pineapples and maraschino cherries, use a 15-oz. can of sliced peaches and reserve ⅓ cup juice for the cake mixture.

SKILLET ROASTED APPLES WITH SALTED CARAMEL SAUCE

The perfect dessert for sharing with family and friends around the campfire.

SERVES 6

PROVISIONS

APPLES

- 1 Tbsp. butter, softened
- 4 large apples, cored and sliced ¼-in. thick
- 1 tsp. ground cinnamon
- 2 Tbsp. melted butter

SALTED CARAMEL SAUCE

- ½ cup sugar
- 2 Tbsp. water
- ¼ cup heavy cream
- 1 Tbsp. butter
- ½ tsp. kosher or sea salt
- Vanilla ice cream or whipped cream, to serve

DIRECTIONS

1. Preheat oven to 425 degrees F.

2. Butter the bottom of a cast-iron skillet with the softened butter. Arrange the apple slices in a concentric circle, overlapping slightly. Sprinkle on the cinnamon and drizzle with melted butter. Cover the pan with foil and roast in the oven for 25 to 30 minutes or until the apples are tender.

3. Make the caramel sauce. Place the sugar and water in a heavy saucepan and cook over medium heat, stirring just until the sugar melts. Once the sugar has melted, do not stir any longer. Cook for about 8 minutes or until the sugar is the color of an old penny. Gently swirl the pan occasionally to ensure even caramelization. Carefully add the cream and whisk until smooth. Remove from the heat and whisk in the butter and salt. Let cool slightly then drizzle over the apples and serve. Top with ice cream or whipped cream if desired.

DID YOU KNOW?

The movie *Allegheny Uprising*, which tells the story of American colonials butting heads with the British, was based on the 1937 novel *The First Rebel*.

John Wayne in *Allegheny Uprising* (1939).

SKILLET TEXAS SHEET CAKE

This dessert comes with a flavor as big and welcoming as the Lone Star state itself.

SERVES 8

PROVISIONS

CAKE

- 1½ cups flour
- ¾ tsp. baking soda
- ¾ tsp. kosher or fine sea salt
- 1½ cups sugar
- 12 Tbsp. butter
- 3 Tbsp. unsweetened cocoa powder
- ½ cup brewed coffee
- ¼ cup water
- ½ cup buttermilk
- 2 tsp. vanilla extract
- 2 large eggs, lightly beaten

FROSTING

- ¼ cup milk
- 4 Tbsp. butter
- 2 Tbsp. unsweetened cocoa powder
- ⅛ tsp. kosher or fine sea salt
- 2 cups powdered sugar
- 1 tsp. vanilla extract
- ½ cup chopped pecans

DIRECTIONS

1. Preheat oven to 350 degrees F.

2. In a medium mixing bowl, whisk together the flour, baking soda and salt.

3. In a 12-in. cast-iron skillet, combine the sugar, butter, cocoa powder, coffee and water. Bring to a boil. Remove from heat and whisk in the dry ingredients. Whisk in the buttermilk, vanilla and eggs. Bake for 20 to 25 minutes or until the cake looks set and a toothpick inserted into the center comes out clean.

4. While the cake is baking, make the frosting. In a small saucepan, combine the milk, butter, cocoa powder and salt. Bring to a boil over medium-high heat. Remove from heat and whisk the powdered sugar in, half a cup at a time. Keep whisking until smooth. Whisk in the vanilla. As soon as the cake is done, spread the frosting over the top in an even layer, sprinkle with the pecans, and let cool at least 10 minutes or until the frosting sets. Can be served warm, at room temperature or cold.

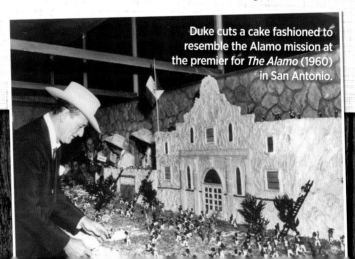

Duke cuts a cake fashioned to resemble the Alamo mission at the premier for *The Alamo* (1960) in San Antonio.

WAYNE FAMILY TIP

If you prefer a stronger coffee flavor in your desserts, use espresso instead of brewed coffee for an extra zing.

S'MORES DIP

This great, gooey dip is perfect for making just about anything more tasty.

SERVES 6 TO 8

PROVISIONS

1   Tbsp. butter

1   (12-oz.) bag semi-sweet chocolate chips

25 large marshmallows, cut in half widthwise

Graham crackers

DIRECTIONS

1. Place a 9-in. cast-iron skillet in the oven and preheat the oven to 450 degrees F. When the oven has preheated, carefully remove the hot pan from the oven, add the butter and swirl the pan to coat with the butter. Add the chocolate chips in an even layer and place the marshmallows in concentric circles over the chocolate. Place back in the oven for 7 to 9 minutes or until the marshmallows are puffed and golden brown. Serve hot with graham crackers for dipping.

DID YOU KNOW?

The last B-Western Duke starred in, *New Frontier*, used stock footage shot for *The Big Trail* (1930), the movie that originally was meant to make John Wayne a star.

John Wayne in
New Frontier
(1939).

SUMMER FRUIT CRISP

A bite of this crisp is like tasting a bright July afternoon.

SERVES 6

PROVISIONS

- 1 cup rolled oats, divided
- ½ cup flour
- ½ cup light brown sugar, lightly packed
- ½ tsp. kosher or fine sea salt
- ½ cup cold butter, cut into small pieces
- ½ cup slivered almonds
- 8 cups mixed berries and stone fruits (peaches, nectarines, plums, cherries) pitted
- 1 cup sugar
- 2 Tbsp. cornstarch
- Juice of 1 lemon
- 1 Tbsp. pure vanilla extract

DIRECTIONS

1. Preheat oven to 350 degrees F.

2. Place ¾ cup oats, flour, brown sugar and salt in a food processor fitted with a steel blade. Process until it resembles coarse crumbs. Add the butter and process until it forms into clumps. Stir in the remaining ¼ cup oats and almond slivers.

3. In a large mixing bowl, combine the fruit, sugar, cornstarch, lemon juice and vanilla. Stir well. Pour the fruit into a cast-iron skillet, crumble the topping over the top and bake for 1 hour. Let cool for about 30 minutes before serving.

John Wayne in "Rookie of the Year," an episode of the televised anthology series *Screen Directors Playhouse*, 1955.

WAYNE FAMILY TIP

Pitting cherries can be a messy task. Try using a chopstick or a plastic drinking straw to cleanly and quickly push out the pits.

BANANAS FOSTER UPSIDE DOWN CAKE

Don't monkey around with this recipe—its intense flavor means business.

SERVES 6 TO 8

PROVISIONS

- 4 Tbsp. cold butter
- ½ cup plus 2 Tbsp. brown sugar, lightly packed
- 1 Tbsp. fresh lemon juice
- 4 tsp. pure vanilla extract, divided
- 3 large bananas, divided
- 1½ cups flour
- 1½ tsp. baking powder
- ½ tsp. kosher or fine sea salt
- ¾ cup sugar
- ½ cup milk
- ½ cup melted butter

DIRECTIONS

1. Preheat oven to 350 degrees F.

2. Combine cold butter and brown sugar in a 9-in. cast-iron skillet, turn the heat to medium-low and cook, stirring until the butter melts. Take off the heat and stir in the lemon juice and 2 tsp. vanilla.

3. Peel two bananas and slice into ¼-in. coins. Carefully place the banana slices in the brown sugar mixture.

4. Combine the flour, baking powder and salt in a large mixing bowl. In another mixing bowl, combine the sugar, milk, melted butter and 2 tsp. vanilla. Combine flour mixture with wet ingredients. Mash the remaining banana well and stir into the batter. Batter will be thick.

5. Spread the batter evenly over the bananas and bake for 30 to 40 minutes or until the cake is golden brown and a toothpick inserted into the center comes out clean. Let cool for 2 to 3 minutes, then run a dinner knife around the edge of the pan, place a serving platter over the skillet and flip it over. If the cake does not come out of the pan, put it back in the oven for a minute or two to heat up the caramel topping.

John Wayne in a scene from *She Wore A Yellow Ribbon* (1949).

DID YOU KNOW?

Actress Mildred Natwick (pictured above) had her first film credit in director John Ford's 1940 film *The Long Voyage Home*, which also starred John Wayne.

John Wayne from *The War Wagon* (1967).

CONVERSION GUIDE

Use this handy chart to convert cups and ounces to liters and grams.

VOLUME

¼ teaspoon	=	1 mL
½ teaspoon	=	2 mL
1 teaspoon	=	5 mL
1 tablespoon	=	15 mL
¼ cup	=	50 mL
⅓ cup	=	75 mL
½ cup	=	125 mL
⅔ cup	=	150 mL
¾ cup	=	175 mL
1 cup	=	250 mL
1 quart	=	1 liter
1½ quarts	=	1.5 liters
2 quarts	=	2 liters
2½ quarts	=	2.5 liters
3 quarts	=	3 liters
4 quarts	=	4 liters

WEIGHT

1 ounce	=	30 grams
2 ounces	=	55 grams
3 ounces	=	85 grams
4 ounces (¼ pound)	=	115 grams
8 ounces (½ pound)	=	225 grams
16 ounces (1 pound)	=	445 grams
1 pound	=	455 grams
2 pounds	=	910 grams

LENGTH

⅛ inch	=	3 mm
¼ inch	=	6 mm
½ inch	=	13 mm
¾ inch	=	19 mm
1 inch	=	2.5 cm
2 inches	=	5 cm

TEMPERATURES

Fahrenheit		Celsius
32°	=	0°
212°	=	100°
250°	=	120°
275°	=	140°
300°	=	150°
325°	=	160°
350°	=	180°
375°	=	190°
400°	=	200°
425°	=	220°
450°	=	230°
475°	=	240°
500°	=	260°

INDEX

Duke and son Patrick on the set of *Hondo* (1953). John Wayne's production company, Batjac Productions, helped create a television series featuring the character of Hondo Lane in 1967.

Media Lab Books
For inquiries, call 646-838-6637

Copyright 2017 Topix Media Lab

Published by Topix Media Lab
14 Wall Street, Suite 4B
New York, NY 10005

Manufactured in Singapore

ISBN-10: 1-942556-92-6
ISBN-13: 978-1-942556-92-3

Recipes and photography by Carol Kicinski. All other photos used with permission of John Wayne Enterprises except: p2 Bettmann/Getty Images; p5 Photo 12/Alamy; p8 Roel Smart/Stocksy; p13 AF Archive/Alamy; p14 Everett Collection Historical/Alamy; p18 Collection Christophel/Alamy; p22 20th Century Fox/Everett Collection; p35 Everett Collection; p36 Glasshouse Pictures/Alamy; p49 Photo 12/Alamy; p57 Interfoto/Alamy; p60 John Springer Collection/Getty Images; p72 ScreenProd/Photononstop/Alamy; p81 Everett Collection; p82 Everett Collection; p89 Entertainment Pictures/Alamy; p90 Everett Collection; p93 Photo 12/Alamy; p94 Everett Collection; p96 Ullstein Bild/Getty Images; p103 ScreenProd/Photononstop/Alamy; p115 Moviestore Collection Ltd/Alamy; p118 Paramount/Getty Images; p125 colaimages/Alamy; p126 SilverScreen/Alamy; p129 Interfoto/Alamy; p130 Everett Collection; p137 Everett Collection; p138 Photo 12/Alamy; p144 debibishop/iStock; p150 Photo 12/Alamy; p154 AF Archive/Alamy; p167 Ronald Grant Archive/Alamy; p175 Collection Christophel/Alamy; p176 Moviestore Collection Ltd/Alamy; p179 Ronald Grant Archive/Alamy; p183 Everett Collection; p184 AF Archive/Alamy; p190 John Springer Collection/Getty Images; p197 Pierluigi Praturlon/Reporters Associati & Archivi/Mondadori Portfolio/Getty Images; p198 Interfoto/Alamy; p201 ScreenProd/Photononstop/Alamy; p205 Ronald Grant Archive/Alamy; p209 Moviestore Collection Ltd/Alamy; p210 Collection Christophel/Alamy; p214 Everett Collection; p217 ScreenProd/Photononstop/Alamy; p226 Everett Collection; p235 Everett Collection; p236 ZumaPress/Alamy; p244 Pictorial Press Ltd/Alamy; Back cover ScreenProd/Photononstop/Alamy

JOHN WAYNE
ENTERPRISES